INSIGHT COMPACT GUIDES

PARIS

Compact Guide: Paris is the ideal companion to the French capital. It tells you everything you need to know about the city's multitude attractions, from the Arc de Triomphe to the Eiffel Tower, from the Louvre to the Moulin Rouge.

This is just one title in *Apa Publications'* new series of pocket-sized, easy·
independent-mind
winning formula
Guides pride ther
authoritative. The
clopedias, designe
both readable and

GW00702902

To: Lesley,

How nice Paris was
and the
train journey!

B.

31.8 / 1.9.95

Star Attractions

An instant reference
to some of Paris's
most popular tourist
attractions to help
you on your way.

Sainte-Chapelle p14

Notre-Dame p18

Musée du Louvre p25

Arc de Triomphe p34

Centre Pompidou p45

Place des Vosges p49

Musée Picasso p50

Montmartre p52

Quartier Latin p55

Eiffel Tower p62

Musée d'Orsay p65

PaRIS

Introduction

Paris – World Metropolis **5**
Historical Highlights **10**

Places

Route 1: Ile de la Cité – Ile Saint-Louis **14**
Route 2: Palais du Louvre **22**
Route 3: Tuileries – Arc de Triomphe **29**
Route 4: Madeleine – Opéra – Palais-Royal **36**
Route 5: Forum des Halles – Centre Pompidou **43**
Route 6: Place de la Bastille – Place des Vosges –
             Musée Picasso **48**
Route 7: Montmartre **52**
Route 8: Quartier Latin – Boulevard St-Germain **55**
Route 9: Eiffel Tower – Musée d'Orsay **61**
Route10: Montparnasse **66**

Additional Sights **69**

Culture

Art History **73**
Music and Theatre **80**

Leisure

Food and Drink **83**
Shopping **85**
Nightlife **87**

Practical Information

Getting There **91**
Getting Around **93**
Facts for the Visitor **97**
Accommodation **102**

Index **104**

Paris – World Metropolis

'Paris', as the Emperor Charles V once said, 'is not a city, it is a world.'

Conquering the nation's capital was always uppermost in the minds of all the powers who warred with France. But it isn't only emperors and kings who have been attracted to Paris; for centuries, painters, sculptors, composers and writers have been drawn to this liberal-minded city: 'If you are lucky enough to have lived in Paris as a young man, then wherever you go for the rest of your life, it stays with you, for Paris is a moveable feast,' wrote Ernest Hemingway.

Magnificent first performances of major works take place regularly in the theatres of the capital, and the city's name has always been linked with innumerable political and cultural events.

A street café

Visitors should not forget that several clichés have given the city a reputation it does not deserve: 'Paris, city of love', 'Paris, city of night-life'. Life here is certainly light-hearted and cheerful, and the city's notorious *savoir vivre* still applies today, just as ever. The Paris behind the tourist facade, however, is a big city like any other and faces difficulties that are often enormously complex.

Paris is a city of enormous wealth and immense poverty. There are worlds between the film star on the Avenue Foch and the tramp rummaging through dustbins beneath the bridges of the Seine. Yet both extremes – the star and the tramp – are still intimately connected with this city in their different ways.

A tour on foot of the various individual *quartiers* is highly recommended; each has its own special atmosphere. Indeed, hardly any one part of Paris resembles any other. New perspectives open up wherever one goes: elegant apartment buildings with magnificent facades on the one hand, and, on the other, ramshackle tenement blocks that have not been painted in decades, let alone refurbished. Paris life gets played out in the rear courtyards, the tiny bistros, in the narrow streets around the former Halles, around the Place de la Bastille and, during the evenings, along the quays of the Seine – these are the places where the contrasts blend into one another.

Location and size

The capital of France lies on roughly the same latitude as Stuttgart in Germany and Vancouver in Canada, at 2°20' east and 48°50' north. Paris is at the centre of the fertile northern French Basin, or more precisely, the Paris Basin.

The Seine runs through the city in a broad arc and connects with the covered stream of the Bièvre in the centre as well as the River Marne (to the east) and the Oise (to

5

the west). It eroded the few remaining tertiary layers here long ago, thus providing a solid basis for the city.

Paris extends from the banks of the Seine up to the chain of hills in the north (Butte Montmartre) and to the south (Butte Ste-Geneviève).

The city's elevation varies between roughly 30m (100ft) on the banks of the Seine in the suburb of Passy and 130m (425ft) at the top of Montmartre.

In terms of surface area, Paris, measuring just 105sq km (40sq miles), is not all that large compared to other world capitals. The city boundary is approximately 36km (22 miles) long. The distance from the west to the east of the city (from the Porte Maillot to the Porte de Vincennes) is 12km (7 miles), and from north to south (from the Porte de Clignancourt to the Porte d'Orléans) nearly 10km (6 miles). The Greater Paris conurbation, which is formed of suburbs and other built-up areas, extends around the city in all directions, covering approximately 2,300sq km (890sq miles).

Covering an area of 12,000sq km (4,637sq miles), the region of Paris-Ile de France consists of the Greater Paris conurbation and the *départements* of Hauts-de-Seine, Val-de-Marne, Essonne, Seine-et-Marne, Seine-Saint-Denis, Val-d'Oise and Yvelines. This catchment area is almost exactly the same size as the US state of Connecticut.

The City

The Seine divides up the city into two unequal parts: the rive droite (the right bank, north of the river) and the rive gauche (the left bank, south of the river). At the centre are the two islands, the Ile de la Cité and the Ile Saint-Louis. The city is intersected by two large series of streets. Forming a long line from north to south are the Boulevard de Strasbourg, Boulevard Sébastopol, Boulevard du Palais and Boulevard St-Michel. The east-west axis is made up of the Rue du Faubourg St-Antoine, Rue de Rivoli, Avenue des Champs-Elysées and the Avenue de la Grande Armée. Then there are the large, ring-shaped boulevards surrounding the actual centre of the city.

The view from Arc de Triomphe

Until the 18th century the sections of the city to the north of the *Grands Boulevards* lay beyond the city wall. Many street names still stand as a reminder of that time. The streets crossing the old border, beyond the *Grands Boulevards*, all contain the word *Faubourg* in their names, which simply means 'suburb' and indicates that a village once stood on that site.

In the *arrondissements* in the city centre and to the east, there is no distinction between office and residential areas: even large office blocks contain private apartments both large and small in their upper storeys. The suburbs to the west and southwest are purely residential, however.

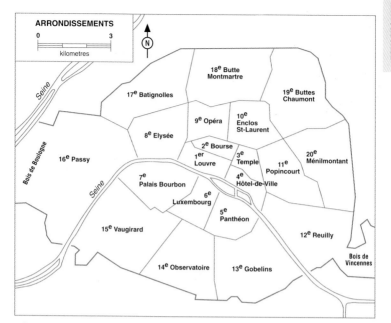

The Seine

The Seine, 766km (475 miles) long, is the longest river in Northern France. Its two banks are connected by 33 bridges in the metropolitan area. The river reaches Paris close to the Bois de Vincennes, just after its confluence with the River Marne. The many moorings for its traffic lie between the Pont National and the Pont d'Austerlitz.

The Pont d'Austerlitz is also the starting-point for the Canal St-Martin, which leads off to the industrial areas in the east. The canal begins at the yacht harbour of Bassin de l'Arsénal and starts off underground, connecting with the harbour of Bassin de la Villette in the 19th *arrondissement*. The latter is connected to the Seine north of Paris by the 6.6-km (4-mile) long Canal St-Denis, and to the Marne via the 10.8-km (7-mile) long Canal de l'Ourcq.

In the centre of the city the Seine flows past its two large islands, Ile de la Cité and Ile Saint-Louis. To the west of the city, near Passy, the Seine flows past another narrow island, the Ile des Cygnes, before leaving the city.

Notre-Dame, Ile de la Cité

Climate

Winter temperatures average 4°C (39°F); summer temperatures occasionally hit 30°C (86°F); spring and autumn are mild with an average of 11°C (52°F). June, September and October are the ideal months for visiting: pleasant and usually sunny, but less crowded than the mid-summer months.

Fun at La Villette

Population

With a population of 2.1 million (not including its sub-urbs), Paris is the seventh largest city in Europe. Sub-urbs included, Paris has a population of over 12 million. Population density in the region is 833 people per square kilometre, and within Paris itself the figure is as high as 20,000 per sq km, making it the most densely populated city in Europe. It contains 3.8 percent of the entire population of France, with one in five French people living in the Paris region. Immigrants make up 12 percent. The population figures for Paris have been steadily receding since 1986, when the rent prices rose dramatically.

The increase in rents has had several other effects, including a sharp rise in the number of homeless; the image of the tramp choosing to live on the streets for more or less intellectual reasons no longer applies. An estimated 20,000 people in Paris at present have nowhere to live. When the weather gets colder, state organisations as well as numerous church charities and private organisations distribute food and clothing; a few Métro stations also stay open in very cold weather, providing the homeless with somewhere to go.

As in many other big cities there are only very few 'genuine natives' to be found in Paris. The typical Parisian has arrived there from the provinces and has usually moved to the city not for any aesthetic reasons, but simply because the French system is so centralised that only the capital offers any chance of a career. For a family in Paris to maintain a reasonable standard of living and also to be able to take advantage of the city's cultural benefits, both parents usually need to have jobs. Young children are thus placed in *crèches* or looked after by foreign *au pairs*; when they get a bit older, all-day school awaits them. Family life takes place at the weekend, usually a long way out of the city in a country retreat. Single people often have to travel large distances at the weekends to visit their families in the provinces.

The pressure to succeed and the hectic pace of city life in Paris are leading to a feeling of ever-increasing isolation, and also to an increase in aggression – particularly noticeable among car drivers. Anyone who has to commute back home to a dreary suburb after a hard day's work, in packed RER and Métro trains, often only experiences Paris as a necessary evil.

St- Pièrre de Montmartre

Religion

Most of the people in Paris are Roman Catholic. The city also has one of the largest Jewish populations in Europe: 200,000. There are only a few Protestants, and Eastern Orthodox believers are a vanishing minority. The city's Islamic population is increasing rapidly, however.

The Paris coat of arms

Economy

The Greater Paris conurbation is the largest industrial centre in France, in nearly every sector. Several characteristically Parisian products enjoy worldwide reputations. Until very recently, this concentration of economic activity resulted in around 23 percent of France's industry being based either in or around Paris. There has been a marked shift into the country's rural regions over the past few years, however – a sign that the rents in Paris are growing ever more unaffordable.

Paris is now the financial centre of the country once again; after Mitterrand put the banks under state control there was a drop in activity in this sector too. In comparison, income from tourism is steadily increasing.

Administration

After the French Revolution of 1789 France was divided up for the first time into 89 Départements plus the Territoire de Belfort (which had the status of a Département). Changes were continually made in the years that followed, more of interest to administrators than to travellers. After the last regional reform, France was divided up into 22 regions with 95 Départements.

The metropolis is divided into 20 *arrondissements* (municipal districts), each run by its own *maire* (mayor). A Paris *arrondissement* is made up of four *quartiers* (quarters). The map on page 7 shows their location. The Louvre *arrondissement* at the centre of Paris is No 1, with the numbers increasing in a clockwise spiral. In colloquial French, only the number of each *arrondissement* is mentioned. On letters it appears at the end of the postcode (ie 75008 means the eighth *arrondissement*). House numbers always start at the part of a street nearest the Seine. In streets parallel to the river the house numbers usually run from east to west.

Historical Highlights

3rd century BC The Celtic tribe of the *Parisii* settles one of the islands in the Seine (known since medieval times as the Ile de la Cité). They found the settlement of *Lucotesia* (Celtic: Midwater-Dwelling) at the centre of the river.

58–52BC Julius Caesar conquers Gaul. Threatened by Roman invasion, the Lucotesians set fire to their settlement and abandon it. At Caesar's command, a typical Roman colonial town is built on the same site: Lutetia.

c AD250 Saint-Denis founds the first Christian community, and is subsequently martyred.

3rd century Germanic tribes cross the Rhine and penetrate Gaul. The Gallo-Roman towns begin building defensive fortifications.

451 Attila the Hun crosses the Danube and the Rhine and heads towards the Loire and the Seine. A nun with the Celtic name of Genoveva (Sainte-Geneviève) urges the people of Paris to resist the invasion. The Huns leave the town intact and are later defeated near Troyes.

486 The Merovingian Clovis (c 466–511) defeats the army of the last Roman governor near Soissons, thus laying the foundation for the first major empire in Europe since antiquity. In 508 Paris becomes the capital of the Frankish Empire.

751–888 Under the Carolingians, Paris loses much of its political importance as the focus shifts to the Rhine, and Aachen, but the city's economic importance increases, with shipping playing a major role. On four occasions, Paris is plundered and destroyed by the Normans. In 885–6, the Robertian Count Eudes withstands a 13-month Norman siege. In 888 he becomes king of the Western Franks at Compiègne.

987 After the death of Louis V, the last Carolingian descendant, Hugh Capet, a Parisian count, is made king, marking the start of the Capetian dynasty, destined to rule France until the revolution. In Paris the upkeep of law and order is entrusted to a provost (prévôt) appointed by the king, who has precedence over judicial and financial administrations. The swamp area to the north is drained, and settlements are created on the right bank.

1108–54 Paris becomes an important trading centre under Louis VI, who campaigns incessantly against the unruly nobility of the Ile de France. Together with his adviser Suger, abbot of Saint-Denis, he re-establishes authority over the royal demesne. His support for schools paves the way for the city's role as capital of science and culture.

In 1154, Henry Plantagenet, ruler of Normandy, Anjou, Poitou and Guienne, is crowned Henry II of England. He wars with Louis VI's successor, Louis VII (1137–80).

1180–1223 Philip II Augustus wins back Plantagenet territory in northern and central France.

1226–70 Under Louis IX 'the Holy', Capetian power is extended as far as the Mediterranean. He removes many of the injustices that had developed under the provosts, and several schools of religious learning are founded in numerous monasteries on the left bank of the Seine.

1328 Philip VI of Valois, grandson of Philip III, becomes king of France. Edward III of England – son of a daughter of Philip the Fair – simultaneously lays claim to the French crown, sparking off the Hundred Years' War, which lasts – with a few interruptions – from 1339 to 1453, when the English are expelled from all France except Calais.

1420 Paris surrenders to the English without a struggle. Nine years later, troops led by Joan of Arc try to retake the city, but without success. Paris is only finally recaptured in 1436.

1572 Under the regency of Catherine de Médicis, the Wars of Religion reach their climax in the Massacre of St Bartholomew's Day (23/24 August), when between 2,000 and 3,000 Protestant Huguenots in Paris are killed by Catholics.

1574–89 The dissolute lifestyle of Henry III, Catherine's youngest son, incurs the wrath of the Parisians. When the Huguenot Henry of Navarre appears on the scene the Catholic League, under Henry of Guise, forms an alliance with the Spanish against the Houses of Valois and Navarre.

Henry III has the Duc de Guise murdered; in 1588 the citizens rebel, and the king is forced to flee. His death – he is stabbed – marks the end of the House of Valois.

1589–1610 Unable to take Paris after a five-year siege, Henry IV of Bourbon-Navarre converts to Catholicism. Henry IV soon proves a capable statesman, and with the aid of his minister Sully succeeds in boosting the economy and increasing state revenues. With the Edict of Nantes (1598) Henry IV allows the Huguenots freedom of religion. After the long siege – during which 13,000 Parisians perish – the city recovers once more.

1610–43 Under Louis XIII, France's *Grand Siècle* (Great Century) begins. Cardinal Richelieu, a minister from 1624, attempts to unite all political power under the king.

1643–1715 King Louis XIV, the Sun King. Civil disturbances by the Frondes force him to flee in 1648 to St-Germain-en-Laye. From 1668 he has his father's hunting-lodge at Versailles extended; in 1682 he shifts the seat of government there.

1789 The Estates-General are called together at Versailles. The Third Estate demands that powers be verified in common. Louis XVI refuses. Troop concentrations result in the citizens of Paris storming the Bastille – the political prison, a symbol of absolutism – on 14 July.

1792–3 On 13 August 1792 the King is arrested, and France is declared a republic on 21 September the same year. The King is guillotined on 21 January 1793.

1799–1814 Napoleon Bonaparte. The first Directory (1795) is followed by the Consulate, with Napoleon as First Consul. On 18 May 1804 he is proclaimed emperor of France by the senate and is anointed by Pope Pius VII on 2 December of the same year in Notre-Dame Cathedral.

1815 After the fall of Napoleon, the Bourbons return to power with the accession of Louis XVIII.

1830–48 After the July Revolution of 1830, Louis-Philippe d'Orléans, the Citizen King, ascends the French throne. He is deposed in the February Revolution of 1848 and the Second Republic is declared. Louis Napoleon, a nephew of Napoleon I, becomes its president.

1852–70 Emperor Napoleon III. After a coup d'état, Louis Napoleon proclaims the Second Empire on 2 December 1852.

1870–71 Franco-Prussian War. The Third Republic is declared on 4 September 1870. Paris capitulates to Prussian siege on 28 January 1871. A rebellion led by a workers' council, the Paris Commune, is bloodily suppressed after several fierce street battles (22–28 May).

1871–1914 Paris soon prospers again. International exhibitions of 1878, 1889 and 1900 draw the world's attention to Paris, which gradually becomes the cultural centre of Europe.

1914–18 World War I. The city is spared from capture thanks to the Battle of the Marne (1914).

1940–4 On 14 June 1940 Paris is captured by German troops without a shot being fired. The Resistance Movement, directed from London by General de Gaulle, becomes increasingly active in Paris, especially in 1944. On 26 August, de Gaulle and the Allied troops enter the liberated city.

1946 Foundation of the Fourth Republic.

1958 After a military coup in Algiers (13 May), the Fifth Republic is declared, with General de Gaulle as its president (until 1969).

1968 In May Paris is rocked by an uprising which swells from student unrest in the Latin Quarter to a nationwide outbreak of strikes.

1969 Les Halles, the centuries-old food market in the middle of Paris, is shifted to Rungis near Orly Airport.

1986 Right-wing parties win elections. Chirac becomes prime minister. Since Mitterrand, the president, is a socialist, a unique situation develops (cohabitation): the country's head of state is not a member of the ruling parties.

1988 Mitterrand reaffirmed as president. The Socialists win elections, bringing the cohabitation to an end.

1992 In regional elections the Front National, a radical right-wing party, and also environmentalist parties, profit from the voters' lack of confidence in the established parties.

1993 Socialists lose elections, but Mitterrand remains President of the Republic.

Sainte-Chapelle, interior
Preceding pages: view of
the Eiffel Tower from the
Palais de Chaillot

On the banks of the Seine

Route 1

★★ **Ile de la Cité** – ★★ **Ile Saint-Louis** (*Métro Pont Neuf, line 7; bus Nos 24, 27, 58, 70, 75*)

The Ile de la Cité is the real heart of Paris. In the 3rd century BC, the Celtic tribe of the *Parisii* built their first huts on this island, the largest in the Seine. In 52BC, Roman legions conquered the settlement and founded *Lutetia Parisiorum* on the left bank.

Despite its name, the massive **Pont Neuf** (New Bridge), built by Henry IV in 1607, is actually the oldest bridge in Paris. It connects the westernmost tip of the island in the Seine with the two banks. The impressive equestrian statue of Henry IV stands on the small square platform between the two arms of the bridge, towering above the Square du Vert-Galant.

Palais de la Cité

This extensive complex of buildings (daily 10am–6pm) on the western end of the island, most of which date from the late 18th and 19th century, contains the remains of the Palais de la Cité, the medieval royal residence with its Gothic Sainte-Chapelle, the Conciergerie and the Palais de Justice (headquarters of France's supreme court).

Access to both the Palais de Justice and the Sainte-Chapelle is via the Cour du Mai, which can be reached from the Boulevard du Palais.

★★★ **Sainte-Chapelle ❶**, the palace chapel, and a masterpiece of Parisian Gothic Rayonnant, once used to stand on its own on the Cour du Mai, connected to the palace via a roofed walkway. Between 1245 and 1248, Louis IX had the chapel converted into an elaborate shrine to house his valuable holy relics. In 1239 he had acquired from the emperor of Byzantium, the Crown of Thorns, believed to be the very one worn by Christ at his crucifixion. Such a priceless treasure had to be very closely guarded, and the king was the only person with a key to the reliquary chapel. Each Good Friday he would display its holy contents to the people in the Cour du Mai but for the rest of the year they were locked away. During the French Revolution the reliquary shrine was melted down to make coins. The Crown of Thorns and part of the True Cross are now in Notre-Dame.

At the beginning of the 19th century the building was used for a while as a powder magazine; restoration work began in 1840.

The exterior of the building – height 36m (120ft), length 17m (55ft) – mainly consists of the high tracery windows of the upper chapel with their pointed gable roofs, and the narrow flying buttresses between them, crowned by tiny finials. The western entrance facade with its large Late Gothic rose window in Flamboyant style is flanked by two Late Gothic towers. The vestibule dates from the year 1850. The Lower Chapel was used by the royal court for prayers. Low lines of columns separate the broad central nave from the noticeably narrow side aisles, and support the ribbed vault. The single-aisled Upper Chapel is a masterpiece of High Gothic architecture: the 13th-century stained glass, magnificently displayed in 85 major panels, is without equal anywhere in Paris. Saint Chapelle is unique amongst Gothic buildings for its medieval frescoes, which have all been restored. The delicately-arcaded apse used to form part of the reliquary altar, and there was once an organ on the western wall.

Stained-glass, Sainte-Chapelle

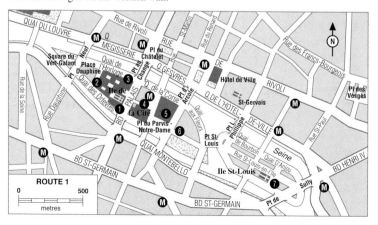

Palais de Justice

Tour d'Horloge

The Palace of Justice, or ★★ **Palais de Justice ❷**, can also be reached via the Cour de Mai. During the French Revolution, the gate leading to the dungeons used to be situated to the right of the flight of steps. It was from here that the condemned were driven to the Place de la Concorde in open carts.

The flight of steps leads up to the front of the building, with its cupola and its allegorical figures, which contains the Galerie Marchande (Merchants' Gallery). Until the revolution this used to be one of the busiest places in Paris; lawyers, judges and their clients would meet here. To the right of it is the Salle des Pas Perdus (Hall of Lost Steps), the former Grande Chambre, and the old palace hall, also known as the Chambre Dorée because of its magnificent decoration (1509). After the fire of 1618 it was rebuilt by Salomon de Brosse as a two-aisled basilica, but assumed its present-day appearance after having been burnt down a second time by the insurrectionary Communards in 1871.

On the left, at the end of the hall, is the courtroom of the first Civil Chamber, still in use today. Once the bedroom of King Louis IX, it was later used by the *parlement*. It was in this chamber that Louis XIV is reputed to have uttered the legendary phrase '*L'etat, c'est moi*' ('I am the state'). The 12-member Revolutionary Tribunal sat in judgement here from 1793. Some 2,700 people were sentenced to death on the guillotine in just 718 days.

On the left, just before the Salle des Pas Perdus, is the Galerie des Prisonniers. The Galerie Saint-Louis, completed in 1877, then leads off to the Galerie Lamoignon.

At the end of this gallery is the Vestibule de Harlay, adorned with statues of famous statesmen (Louis IX, Philip II Augustus, Napoleon I). The Galérie de la Première Présidence with the Cour d'Appel (Court of Appeal) leads on to the exit.

At the corner of the Palais de Justice – still on the Boulevard du Palais – a further three towers dating from the 14th century can be seen alongside the **Tour d'Horloge**: the Tour de César, the Tour d'Argent and the Tour Bonbec. These were all originally built for defensive purposes, but were later used to house the royal treasury and for a time as a torture chamber. The Tour d'Horloge contains the city's very first tower-clock, built by the German clockmaker Heinrich von Vic in 1370.

To the left of the Tour de César is the entrance to the ★★ **Conciergerie ❸**. After the royal residence was moved to the Louvre in 1358, during the reign of Charles V, the palace was entrusted to a royal caretaker (concierge). The ground floor of the Conciergerie was already being used as a state prison as early as 1400. Among those who languished here were Montgomery, who fatally wounded

King Henry II during a tournament in 1559, Ravaillac, who murdered King Henry IV in 1610, and also the famous robber Cartouche (1693–1721). During the French Revolution, the Conciergerie was turned into a kind of waiting-room for the condemned. Up to 1,200 prisoners were held here before being carted off to the guillotine. Among them were Marie-Antoinette, Madame Dubarry, Charlotte Corday, the poet André Chénier, and later Danton and Robespierre. Part of the Conciergerie is still in use as a remand prison today.

The tour of the building begins at the Cour d'Entrée. The first room is the Salle des Gardes (guardroom), in use as early as the 14th century. On the Rue de Paris, where up to 200 people awaited execution during the revolution, lies the Salle des Gens d'Armes, a huge Gothic hall – 70m (230ft) x 30m (100ft) – one of the mightiest secular structures of the Middle Ages. It was built during the reign of Philip IV (1285–1314), and served as a banqueting hall and recreation room for the royal household.

The palace kitchen

17

On the northern side of the hall a free-standing spiral staircase and a passageway lead to the ★ **palace kitchen**, or Cuisine St-Louis, built in around 1353; it has a huge open fireplace in each of its four corners, and each of them had a special function (one for frying, one for baking, etc). This is where the meals for the whole royal household, roughly 3,000-strong, were prepared. At the end of the Rue de Paris is the section of the prison, reconstructed in 1989, that was used during the French Revolution. The lodges on either side of the entrance belonged to the guards and to the 'clerk', and a little further on to the left is the Salle de la Toilette, where the prisoners were prepared for execution.

Replica of Marie-Antoinette's cell

The upper storey contains the cells occupied by the more 'privileged' prisoners as well as a room bearing the names of every single one of the 2,780 people executed during the French Revolution. Passing a small exhibition documenting the history of the place one arrives at a stairway leading down to the Chapelle des Girondins, in which the moderate Girondins who supported Danton spent their last hours. Marie-Antoinette was imprisoned here from 11 September 1793 until her execution on 16 October of the same year, in a small cell that used to be behind the altar.

The starting-point of the tour is reached once more by crossing the Cour des Femmes; a reconstruction of Marie-Antoinette's cell can be seen on the left.

Keeping guard

On the other side of the Boulevard du Palais, the headquarters of the Paris police, the **Préfecture de Police** ❹, is also that of Interpol; Simenon's *Maigret* detective stories have made the **Quai des Orfèvres** very familiar to all crime film fans.

At the Marché aux Fleurs

Place du Parvis Notre-Dame

Main portal detail, Notre-Dame

The most charming flower market (**Marché aux Fleurs**) in all Paris takes place here every day (except Sunday) beneath the imposing facades of the administrative buildings on the Place Louis-Lépine, between the Tribunal de Commerce and the Hôtel-Dieu. On quiet Sunday mornings there is a bird market (**Marché aux Oiseaux**) held here instead.

Right next to the Place Louis-Lépine is the enormous complex of buildings forming the **Hôtel-Dieu ❺**, the hospital that was built between 1866 and 1878. A hospital of the same name existed here in medieval times. A convent was founded on the site in the 7th century and the nuns devoted themselves to caring for the sick and needy.

The square in front of Notre-Dame, the **Place du Parvis Notre-Dame**, was once much smaller. The bishops held their Court of Inquisition here during the Middle Ages. The square owes its present-day appearance to Haussmann (*see page 35*). Excavations have revealed traces of Gallo-Roman and Early Medieval Paris, including the 6th-century Merovingian cathedral of St-Etienne.

We now come to ★★★ **Notre-Dame ❻**. This huge cathedral dominates the city, and is still its spiritual and architectural centrepiece. 'The cathedrals are France itself', in the words of sculptor Auguste Rodin. Among those cathedrals, Notre-Dame in particular is not only the symbol of Paris but of the whole of France, and is closely connected with the most important events of the nation's past. Construction work on the cathedral began in 1163, and actually finished around 1240, but additions and extensions were then made which took a further 80 years to complete.

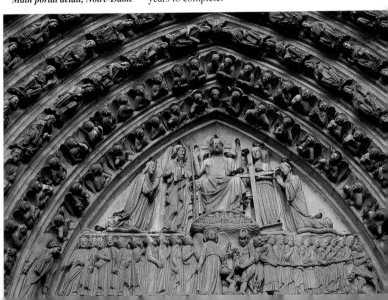

The exterior – west front

The scale of Notre-Dame exceeded all earlier churches. Paris became the capital only a few years before the foundation stone was laid, and the building was designed to reflect the power of the state and its church.

The lower storey with its smooth walls and pillars is reminiscent of the Romanesque style. Above it is the King's Gallery (c 1220, copied by later cathedrals). The storey with the Rose Window was probably inspired by the one at Laon cathedral. The towers above are connected by a terrace (providing a superb view of the city) enclosed by a balustrade. There are also tiny sentry-boxes up here (Tower: 10am–5pm; closed public holidays and 1 January, 1 May, 14 July and 25 December.

Just as Gothic cathedrals were considered symbols of paradise, so the entrance facade, with its series of sculptures, was considered to be the gateway to heaven. The original cycle of figures was partially damaged during the revolution (the fragments are on display in the Musée de Cluny). Numerous sculptures from St Mary's portal on the far left date from 1220–40. The figures on the section of doorway, restored in the 19th century, surrounding the statue of the Virgin, include two saints very closely associated with Paris: St-Denis and Ste-Geneviève. The Judgement Portal in the middle shows Christ at the Last Judgement in the centre of the tympanum with two angels, and the kneeling figures of Mary Magdalene and John the Baptist, interceding for poor souls. The two rows of figures on the door lintel below again portray the Last Judgement. The figures of Christ and the Apostles are 19th-century reconstructions. On the right-hand side is St Anne's Portal. The figures on the lintel and the tympanum (1150–65) were probably constructed for the building that formerly stood on the site, the cathedral of St-Etienne. Along with a few remains found in 1977, they are the oldest masterpieces of Gothic art in Paris.

The famous gargoyles, which resemble mythical creatures, are the imaginative work of Viollet-le-Duc, who restored the cathedral in the 19th century.

Photographers like the gargoyles

North transept – facade

The name of the architect who designed the facade for the cathedral's north transept survives to this day in an inscription on the southern arm: Jean de Chelles. Like the Sainte-Chapelle constructed shortly before it, the facade (c 1250) represents the second style of Parisian Gothic. The portal and the two fake portals on either side of it are crowned by pointed triangles of stone with charming finials between them. On the portal pillar is a statue of the Virgin – the only original work preserved here – with marvellous flowing contours.

North transept facade

South transept – facade

The portal is consecrated to St-Etienne, the patron saint of the Merovingian structure that formerly stood on the site. Sculptured figures on the portal recount his life and martyrdom. The statues of the Apostles and of St-Etienne are copies of the originals, which were damaged.

The interior

The nave

The mighty interior of this Early Gothic church with its five naves is shrouded in a mystical half-light. The side-aisles, broken up by the transepts which are hardly any higher than the nave, continue on into the choir as a double ambulatory. Additional chapels are attached to the outer side-aisles; the choir chapel was originally constructed at the end of the 13th century. The interior elevation of the centre aisle wall (reconstructed in the area of the crossing by Viollet-le-Duc in the 19th century) was formerly four storeys high and is also Early Gothic, as are the sturdy round columns of the arcade and the sexpartite ribbed vault above the centre aisle – replaced in the High Gothic period (at the time Chartres was built) by an oblong rib vault over one bay, and continuing wall shafts down to the base of the piers.

Windows

The northern rose window

In the 18th century the cathedral's windows were enlarged, but it was still too gloomy, and so in 1756 the medieval stained glass was replaced by brighter panes. Only the rose windows were allowed to retain their original colours. The western rose window (c 1230) shows the Virgin at its centre. Surrounding her are kings, virtues and vices, months of the year and signs of the zodiac. The Virgin is also at the centre of the northern rose window (c 1250), this time in the company of figures and scenes from the Old Testament. The southern rose window (c 1270) shows Christ surrounded by apostles and martyrs.

Furnishings

The cathedral interior was ransacked during the revolution. The choir stalls and a few memorial slabs are all that remain of its medieval furnishings. The Statue of the Virgin, on the southeastern pillar of the crossing, is Gothic and is said to work miracles. The Gothic high altar fell victim to baroque modernisation during the reign of Louis XIV. There are also several very interesting large-format paintings (17th-century) in the nave chapels.

Finally there is the **Mémorial de la Déportation**. This memorial (by G H Pingusson, 1962) on the Square de l'Ile de France stands as a reminder of the many French Jews who died in German concentration camps.

★★ Ile St-Louis

The quiet quays of this little island in the Seine can be reached via the pedestrian footbridge of Pont St-Louis. It is certainly worthwhile taking a stroll along the narrow streets here, past the elegant facades and the quiet inner courtyards behind them.

Organ grinder

The Ile St-Louis originally consisted of two mudbanks owned by the cathedral chapter that were handed over by royal command in 1614. After the channel dividing them had been filled in, the new island thus formed then had its circumference diked and was connected to the shore via two bridges. From 1618, craftsmen began to settle there, and in 1638 the island became a popular building site for rich nobles, who erected their *hôtels* here to escape the unhealthy confines of the city centre. One such building is the Hôtel Chenizot at No 51, Rue St-Louis en l'Ile, with its rococo facade.

Also in the same street is the church of **St-Louis-en-L'Ile** ❼. The architect of this church, built in 1664, was Le Vau, one of those responsible for the design of Versailles. The church was only completed in 1725, however, long after Le Vau's death in 1670. The side tower was added later, in 1765. The interior, designed according to a cruciform ground-plan, consists of a barrel-vaulted nave and accompanying side-aisles.

21

The **Hôtel de Lambert** (2 Rue St-Louis-en-L'Ile) was built by Le Vau, an advisor to Louis XIV. It was constructed between 1640 and 1652 for the president of the *parlement* at that time, Lambert de Thorigny, and is probably the most important palais on the island, though its uncomplicated exterior gives one no idea of the sheer wealth of decoration within. Voltaire (1694–1778) used to live here at one time. In the 19th century, it was a popular meeting place for artists.

Detail, Hôtel Lauzun

On the Quai d'Anjou lies the **Hôtel Lauzun**, its Louis XIV interior decoration still almost entirely intact. As with other *hôtels* along the quays of the Ile St-Louis, the reverse of the usual Paris ground-plan is noticeable: the Corps de Logis is on the Seine side, with the courtyard and outbuildings behind it. Le Vau was also responsible for this palace, which belonged to the Richelieu family at one time. In the mid-19th century that eccentric pair, Charles Baudelaire and Théophile Gautier lived here too. The house has been the property of the city since 1928, and can be visited on Saturday and Sunday afternoons from April to October.

Evening time, Ile St-Louis

Plaques on several of the houses bear the names of the famous people who once lived on the island. Many of them were magistrates and financiers, who are hardly household names today, but André Breton (1896–1966) was one resident whose name is familiar to everyone.

Views of the glass pyramid, Palais du Louvre

The castle's foundations

Route 2

★★ **Palais du Louvre** (*Métro Palais-Royal – Musée du Louvre (lines 1 and 7); bus Nos 21, 67, 69, 72, 76, 85, 95*).

The oldest and probably the most lavish museum in the world is in the process of being turned into the largest in the world. Over the centuries, the Louvre has served at various times as a fortress, a prison, a palace for the kings of France, an administration centre, an academy and, most recently, an art gallery and museum.

The museum has been extended. The first construction phase on the Grand Louvre (the main entrance with the pyramid, underground car park, reception rooms, concert hall and restaurant) has been completed, and the finance ministry has moved out of the Richelieu wing, the museum will be extended to fill the rooms thus vacated. The redevelopment work, which on completion will have provided the Louvre with a full 6ha (14.8 acres) of exhibition space, is due to end in 1994.

The main entrance is the controversial **glass pyramid** by American architect Ieoh Ming Pei; it also forms part of the city's 'royal axis' that runs from the Cour Carrée of the Louvre past the obelisk on the Place de la Concorde and the Arc de Triomphe all the way to the Grande Arche in La Défense.

A crusader castle, with round corner-towers and a 32-m (100-ft) high keep, was built as a bulwark beside the Seine during the reign of Philip II Augustus (1180–1223). It contained the state treasure, the city archives and the armoury. The castle's foundations were only discovered very recently, in 1984, beneath today's Cour Carrée (access via the main entrance below the pyramid).

Charles V had the city walls extended in 1370, and the Louvre then lost its military importance. The king had windows built into the fortress, housed his library in one of the towers and during the last years of his regency (until 1380) he turned the Louvre into a magnificent residence.

During the Hundred Years' War the Louvre stood empty. It was only during the reign of Francis I that the residence returned here, and in the last year of his reign work began on converting the building into the Italian Renaissance style. The architect he commissioned to do the work was Pierre Lescot (1510–78). Francis' successors Henry II, Henry III and Henry IV extended the building still further. Cathérine de Medicis (1564–72), for instance, after the death of her husband Henry II, had a palace built 500m (1600ft) west of the Louvre on the site of a former tilery (Tuileries). The building was rectangular-shaped, with central and side pavilions. The plan was to join the Louvre and the Tuileries Palace together. A first step in that direction was taken during Cathérine's time: the Petite Galerie. Under Henry IV the Grande Galerie (1595–1608) was built along the Seine, a long, two-storey connecting section with arcades facing the courtyard side and a closed ground-floor facade facing the Seine. After the death of Henry IV – the only king to die in the Louvre – his widow, Marie de Médicis, built the Palais du Luxembourg. In 1661 Louis XIV rejected a design by Bernini for the east front, and a neoclassical colonnade by Parisian doctor Claude Perrault was chosen in preference. In 1673 construction work started, but there was not enough money to complete the project – mainly due to the decision to build Versailles. After the royal court had moved there, the Louvre remained incomplete. The east and north wings

View of the Grande Galerie

23

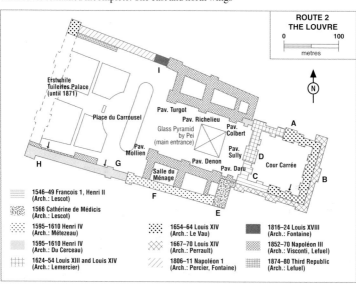

ROUTE 2
THE LOUVRE

0   100

metres

N

Erstwhile Tuileries Palace (until 1871)

Place du Carrousel

Pav. Turgot

Pav. Richelieu

Glass Pyramid by Pei (main entrance)

Pav. Colbert

Pav. Mollien

Pav. Sully

A

Pav. Denon

Pav. Daru

D

Cour Carrée

Salle du Ménage

C

B

H

G

F

E

I

	1546–49 Francois 1, Henri II (Arch.: Lescot)
	1566 Cathérine de Médicis (Arch.: Lescot)
	1595–1610 Henri IV (Arch.: Métezeau)
	1595–1610 Henri IV (Arch.: Du Cerceau)
	1624–54 Louis XIII and Louis XIV (Arch.: Lemercier)

	1654–64 Louis XIV (Arch.: Le Vau)
	1667–70 Louis XIV (Arch.: Perrault)
	1806–11 Napoléon 1 (Arch.: Percier, Fontaine)

	1816–24 Louis XVIII (Arch.: Fontaine)
	1852–70 Napoléon III (Arch.: Visconti, Lefuel)
	1874–80 Third Republic (Arch.: Lefuel)

The Cour Carrée

had no roofs, and the colonnade was only completed in 1755. After the king had moved out, the newly-founded academies were transferred there.

In 1783 the Grande Galerie was converted into a museum, and its existence was confirmed by the revolution in 1793 as Musée Central des Arts. Its contents were extended by the addition of items from the other royal palaces (with the exception of Versailles). Napoleon's court architects Percier and Fontaine added a third storey to the wings around the Cour Carrée. Napoleon also completed the connection to the Tuileries, where he himself lived. Last but not least, in 1852 Napoleon III had Visconti erect two symmetrical sections, built around a number of courtyards, between the Louvre and the gallery buildings. The library was housed in the north wing, and the south wing contained staterooms. The Tuileries Palace was badly damaged by the insurrectionists of the Commune in 1871. In 1882 what remained of it was completely demolished except for two corner pavilions.

The exterior

The tour around the outside of the Louvre begins in the Rue de Rivoli, at the Pavillon Marengo [**A**]: the north facade is undecorated except for the tympanum, with its reliefs of trophies and weapons (17th-century).

The facade of the Pavillon St-Germain-l'Auxerrois [**B**] is French neoclassical baroque. Above the huge gable windows are medallions bearing the initials of Louis XIV. The tympanum of the centre pavilion shows a neoclassical Minerva with a bust of the Sun King (by le Mot, 1811).

Statue of Mazarin on the Lescot facade

Access to the inner courtyard of the Louvre, or Cour Carrée, is via the east portal. In the southwest corner of this, the oldest part of the palace, the outlines of the castle dating from the time of Philip II Augustus can be seen on the ground. Towering above is the facade [**C**] by Pierre Lescot, considered one of the finest works of the French Renaissance.

The Palais de l'Horloge [**D**] dominates the centre of the west front. The caryatids (1636) on the uppermost floor, arranged in pairs, have often been copied.

From the Petite Galerie [**E**], built for Cathérine de Médicis in 1566, proceed to the Grande Galerie or Galerie du Bord de l'Eau [**F**]; the facade along its eastern section as far as the Pont du Carroussel (1595–1608) is the only part that is original. The initials H and G on the facade are those of Henry IV, who built it, and of his favourite mistress Gabrielle d'Estrées. The eastern part of the building ends with the Passage des Guichets [**G**], giving access to the Place du Carroussel.

The group of figures portraying the triumph of the goddess of spring, up on the tympanum of the Pavillon de Flore

[**H**], the former corner pavilion of the Tuileries Palace, is particularly fine. A gateway at the Pavillon de Rohan [**I**] opens out into the Rue de Rivoli.

In the Cour Napoléon is the 19-m (62-ft) high glass pyramid by the architect I M Pei (1988), covering the central entrance area to the Grand Louvre and filling its hall with daylight. Architecture old and new combines here to form a tense unity. A car park and a shopping arcade are being constructed beneath the Cour du Carroussel.

The main entrance under the pyramid can be reached from the Métro station Palais-Royal–Musée du Louvre via the Pavillon Richelieu. There is also a second entrance in the Pavillon de Flore.

★★★ Musée du Louvre

Inside the glass pyramid

Because of refurbishment, some exhibition rooms have been temporarily closed and several works of art have been 'reshuffled' for a time, or cannot be inspected. The central information desk in the entrance hall provides a pamphlet to keep visitors abreast of the changes (daily except Tuesday 9am–6pm, Monday and Thursday until 9.45pm; closed on public holidays).

In the Galerie d'Apollon

The three wings of the museum (*Richelieu* in the north, *Sully* in the east and *Denon* in the south), are divided into 10 so-called *arrondissements*; numbering begins in the Richelieu wing.

The new rooms of the Richelieu wing were completed in November 1993. In both the Sully and Denon wings, conversion work is expected to continue until 1997, and some rooms are bound to be closed from time to time.

The collections are spread over seven different sections, each assigned its own colour to facilitate orientation. The following is a selection of the real highlights from the various different sections (a catalogue in English is available from the bookshop in the entrance area).

Ancient Civilisations section (yellow)

Begins on the mezzanine floor of Richelieu, continues on the ground floor and then on the ground floor of Sully.

Archaeological evidence of the oldest human civilisations of Mesopotamia, 4th–1st millennium BC.

Sumer: 'Vulture stele' of a Sumerian king, c 265BC; early writings including clay tablets of priests from Uruk, 2nd millennium BC.

Mari and Larsa: Seated statue of a royal official, first half of 3rd millennium BC.

Babylon: Basalt block with the oldest legal codex in the world (1800BC).

Assyria: Fragments of wall reliefs, stone guardians in the form of winged bulls and the giant Gilgamesh from the royal palaces at Khawsarbad and Nineveh (8–700BC).

Egyptian relief

Susa: Early ceramics (4th millennium BC); capitals from the palace of Artaxerxes II.

Mediterranean regions: Finds from Phoenicia, Palmyra, Cyprus, Doura-Europus and Ras Shamra in Syria, etc.

Egyptian section (green)

Begins in Sully floors 5 and 6.

Thinite Empire (3330–2778BC): Exhibits including statues of husband and wife, Sepa and Nesa (c 2750BC); stele of King Djet with Horus falcon (c 3000BC).

Old Kingdom (2723–2242BC): Tomb from Saqquarah, statue of a scribe.

Middle Kingdom (2060–1785BC): Black granite statue of King Sesostris III, wood sculpture and sarcophagus of Chancellor Nakhti, huge statue of Sethosis II.

New Kingdom (1580–1090BC): Black sarcophagus of Ramses III with reliefs, paintings from the tomb of King Sethos I in the Valley of the Kings showing the king with the goddess Hathor.

Coptic art (AD300–400): Early examples of Christian art in Egypt from the monastery at Bawit.

Jewellery, artefacts and utensils from the various Egyptian Kingdoms.

A 4,000-year-old scribe

Greek, Etruscan and Roman Antiquity section (blue)

Begins in Denon floor 8, continues on floors 7 and 1.

The Louvre's collection of Greek and Roman art dates back to Francis I, who had casts made from antique originals for his palaces. Cardinal Mazarin and Louis XIV also organised the large-scale purchase of antique originals. The collection has been considerably extended now through the generous purchase of major private collections and the transfer of European art treasures from the lands once occupied by Napoleon.

Galerie Campana: This collection of Greek vases documents the development of the geometrical style until the 4th century BC.

Archaic Hall: Original Greek statues from the early period of Greek sculpture (7th and 6th century BC).

Parthenon Hall: Greek originals from the Classical Period of the 5th century.

Phidias Hall: Roman copies of statues and reliefs by Phidias (alongside Polyclitus the main exponent of high Classical Greek sculpture).

Polyclitus Hall: Originals and copies by contemporaries and successors of Phidias.

Praxiteles Hall: The Louvre contains the best collection of Roman copies based on the work of this Late Classical master of the 4th century.

Hall of the Venus de Milo: This ancient statue of Aphrodite (2nd century BC) was found on the Aegean island of Melos in 1820.

Venus de Milo

Following these are the Halls of *Lysippus*, of the *Greek Poets* and of *Alexander*, and the *Corridor of Pan*.

Rotonde d'Anne d'Autriche: A round hall with portraits of philosophers and the *Borghese Vase*, after which the relief vases in the park at Versailles were modelled.

27

There then follows a hall with *Hellenistic* and *Roman reliefs*, the *Vestibule of the Captured Barbarians* and also the *Cour du Sphinx* with monumental fragments from Greek and Roman tombs and other sacred structures.

The *Roman portrait sculpture* section takes up six halls and provides a good overall impression of the style.

Daru Stairwell: This room contains what is probably the greatest masterpiece of Greek sculpture in the world: the *Winged Victory of Samothrace* (c 200BC).

The *Salle des Bijoux* is followed by the *Etruscan Hall* with its terracotta sarcophagus of a married couple.

By 1997 the mezzanine floor of Denon 8 will house a *Circuit des trois antiquités*, where selected exhibits from the three antiquity sections will provide a summary of Mediterranean culture of late Antiquity.

Winged Victory of Samothrace

European Sculpture section (light blue)

The European sculpture section is divided into French, Italian and 'Northern' sculpture.

French sculpture from 12th–19th century: Richelieu floors 2 and 3, around the two covered courtyards Cour de Marly and Cour de Puget. Highlights of the collection are the 16th-century *Horses of Marly* as well as an important selection of sculptures from the 18th and the beginning of the 19th century.

Italian sculpture from 13th–17th century: Denon 9, mezzanine and ground floors: Collection includes Michelangelo's *Slaves*.

Northern sculpture: Denon 9, mezzanine and ground floors: numerous late-Gothic pieces from German-speaking countries.

Crafts section (purple)

Medieval art: Richelieu 1–3, floor 1: notable royal insignia and treasure from the Abbey of St Denis, as well as Renaissance tapestries.

17th- and 18th-century crafts: Sully 4 and 5, floor 1 (only until 1995).

Painting section (red)

French painting: begins in Richelieu 3, floor 2 and continues in Sully 5–7, floor 2; the large format paintings of the 19th century remain in Denon 8 and 9, floor 1. 15th-century (including Avignon School); 16th-century including Jean Clouet (portraits of *Francis I* and *Elisabeth of Austria*); 17th-century includes Louis le Nain, Nicolas Poussin, Claude Lorrain, Philippe de Champaigne; 18th-century works by Antoine Watteau, Jean-Baptiste Chardin, François Boucher; 19th-century includes J-L David, D Ingres, T Géricault, E Delacroix and G Courbet.

da Vinci's masterpiece, Mona Lisa

Italian painting: nearly the whole of floor 1 of Denon (8–10): medieval, including Cimabue and Simone Martini; Renaissance, including Paolo Uccello, Giovanni Bellini, Correggio, Paolo Veronese, Caravaggio; also Leonardo da Vinci's *Mona Lisa*.

Dutch painting: Richelieu 1–3, floor 2: 15th- and 16th-century: Jan van Eyck, Rogier van der Weyden, Hans Memling, Quentin Massys, Jean Gossaert, Frans Hals, Rembrandt, Jacob van Ruisdael, Vermeer.

Flemish painting: Richelieu 1–3, floor 2: including Jan Breughel, Peter Paul Rubens, Jacob Jordaens, Anton van Dyck; Galérie Médicis: cycle of paintings by Rubens glorifying the life of Maria de Médicis.

Spanish painting: Denon 10, floor 1: includes El Greco, Giuseppe de Ribera, Murillo, Velázquez and Goya.

Old German painting: Richelieu 3, floor 2: Including Albrecht Dürer, Lucas Cranach the Elder, Johann Friedrich von Sachsen, Hans Holbein the Younger.

English 18th-century painting: Richelieu 3, floor 2: including portraits by Lawrence, Gainsborough and Reynolds.

Musée des Arts de la Mode

The Pavillon de Marsan has housed the Museum of Fashion since 1986 (109 Rue de Rivoli). Here the history of fashion from 1780 to the present is documented in a collection assembled by leading fashion designers. The Museum of Decorative Arts (Musée des Arts Décoratifs) is situated next door.

From the Museum of Decorative Arts

Route 3

★★ Tuileries – ★★ Arc de Triomphe *(Métro Palais-Royal or Tuileries (line 1); bus Nos 68, 69, 72)*

Between the Louvre and the Place de la Concorde is the **Jardin des Tuileries** ❽, which Cathérine de Médicis originally laid out in front of her palace in Renaissance style after the death of her husband. In 1664, landscape architect Le Nôtre was given the task of enlarging and redesigning the Tuileries Gardens. He laid out a parterre, and livened it up with two small pools and one large one containing fountains, which formed the focal point of the geometrically-designed gardens. The Jardin des Tuileries only began to be decorated with statues in the 18th century. Artistically the most valuable of the numerous sculptures came from the then dilapidated Château de Marly. The sculptures around the large octagonal pond, all of them the work of Coustou and van Cleve, are artistically important: hermae representing the four seasons, recumbent river gods based on antique models and female allegories representing French rivers.

In the Jardin des Tuileries

Statue in the Tuileries

29

On the north side of the Louvre and the Jardin des Tuileries is the **Rue de Rivoli**, its name a reminder of Napoleon's victory over the Austrians at Rivoli (north of Verona) in 1797. After over 500 houses were torn down in 1811, construction work finally started on this street. The work was only completed in 1833, however – long after the emperor's abdication in 1814.

The straight line of this street and the regimented design of the facades bordering it have been traditional in Paris ever since the time of Henry IV and Louis XVI. The arcaded passageways now contain luxury shops, cafés and bookstores.

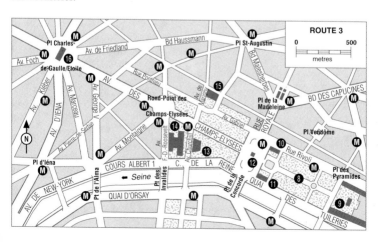

In 1944 General von Choltitz, placed in charge of Paris by Hitler, set up his headquarters in the Hôtel Meurice (No 228). The general prevented the destruction of the city by refusing to carry out the Fuehrer's orders for all the bridges, monuments and important buildings in the city to be blown up during the German retreat.

It was a street which attracted a number of famous residents including the Russian novelist Ivan Turgenev (1818–83) who lived here with his daughter (at No 210). French author Alexandre Dumas, Père (1802–70) also lived at No 22 Rue de Rivoli in 1836.

The indoor riding arena of the Tuileries used to stand between the Rue de Castiglione and the Place des Pyramides. The Constituent Assembly set up an assembly hall there in 1789, and the First Republic was declared there on 21 September 1792.

Detail, Arc de Triomphe du Caroussel

★ **Arc de Triomphe du Carroussel 9**. This triumphal arch stands as a *point de vue* to the east of the Jardin des Tuileries. Work began on it in the same year as the Arc de Triomphe de l'Etoile – 1806 – and like its larger namesake it was intended to glorify the victorious campaigns of Napoleon. It was designed by imperial architects La Fontaine and Percier, and was a neoclassical copy of the Roman triumphal arch for Septimius Severus and Constantine. The arch with its three gateways (19.5m/64ft wide, 14.6m/48ft high) forms the entrance to the courtyard of the Tuileries, and was consecrated in 1808. It was originally crowned by the four bronze horses from San Marco in Venice (they had been brought back to Paris as booty). The present four horses are the work of Bosio, and were placed there in 1828.

The large statues above the main cornice show Napoleonic soldiers wearing the uniforms of the different army corps. The inscriptions at the top of the arch were composed by the emperor, priding himself on having liberated the vanquished peoples. The Arc de Triomphe du Carroussel is a harmonious edifice, enlivened by its high-quality neoclassical relief decoration illustrating the Napoleonic campaigns. Ever since the Tuileries Palace was pulled down in 1882, however, the arch has looked somewhat forlorn, stuck in the middle of the large open space between the Louvre and the Jardin des Tuileries. Nevertheless, the view through the arch across the Place de la Concorde and all the way to the Arc de Triomphe de l'Etoile is unique. The end of the axis is formed by the Grande Arche de la Défense, which is more than twice as high as the Arc de Triomphe.

Maillol sculpture

The area where the Tuileries Palace used to stand, between the Pavillon Marsan and the Pavillon de Flore, is now an open-air museum containing sculptures by Aristide Maillol, produced between 1900 and 1938.

Monet's 'Les Nymphéas'

Jeu de Paume . Napoleon III had this built as an indoor court for royal tennis, and also constructed a hothouse opposite it, known as the Orangerie. The latter has housed the National Gallery for Contemporary Art since June 1991.

★★ **Orangerie** ⓫. Don't miss Claude Monet's world-famous paintings of water-lilies on the lower floor. The great Impressionist painter captured the play of colour on the water-lily pond in his Japanese garden at Giverny at varying times of day.

Busking is big in Paris

On the occasion of the Treaty of Aachen in 1748, which ended the Austrian War of Secession, Paris decided to honour King Louis XV with an equestrian statue. In 1755, construction work duly began on the imposing square ★★ **Place de la Concorde** ⓬, based on plans by the architect Gabriel. The royal square in which the statue of Louis XV and two fountains were erected took the form of a rectangle with the edges rounded off, surrounded by balustrades and water-free ditches. The top storeys of the two large buildings to the north of the square carry on the theme of the Louvre colonnade, and are closed off at the side by gabled corner pavilions. The monument to the king was erected in 1763, and the square was duly consecrated as the Place Louis XV on order of the city senate. In 1792 the square was renamed Place de la Révolution, and the equestrian statue of the king was melted down to make copper coins.

Plaque to Louis XVI and Marie-Antoinette, Place de La Concorde

On the northern side of the square where today the Statue of the City of Brest stands, Louis XVI was executed on 21 January 1793. Later the guillotine was shifted to the entrance to the Tuileries. According to official estimates, 1,119 people were decapitated here including Charlotte Corday, the Girondist leader, Queen Marie-Antoinette, Prince Philippe, Madame Dubarry, André Chénier and Robespierre. During the Directory in 1795 the square received its present-day name: Concord Square. During the reign of King Louis-Philippe (1830–48) the Cologne architect Hittorf began redesigning it, and the work was finally completed in 1854.

Since 1836 the centre of the square has been dominated by the almost 23-m (75-ft) high obelisk from Luxor, presented to Louis-Philippe (1830–48) by the Ottoman governor of Egypt (Mehmed Ali) in 1831. This almost 3,200-year-old pink granite monolith (it weighs around 230 tons) formerly stood in front of the Temple of Luxor. Hieroglyphs proudly recount the deeds of Ramses II. The two fountains (also designed by Hittorf) on the left and right of the obelisk are modelled after those of St Peter's Square in Rome. The horsebreakers by Coustou (1745) were originally destined for the nearby Château de Marly. In 1798 they were positioned at the start of the Champs-Elysées, near the entrance to the Tuileries Gardens, as a counterpiece to the groups displaying Renommée, the goddess of fame, and the god Mercury on winged horses, both by Coysevox (1702).

Mercury on his winged horse

The Place de la Concorde provides the most magnificent view of the ★★ **Champs-Elysées** as far as the Arc de Triomphe. This splendid avenue is considered by many – not only the French – to be the finest in the world. It provides a grand scenario for parades and other national events. Millions stroll up and down this 1.9-km (1.1-mile) long boulevard every year. However, from the early hours of the morning until late into the night the Champs-Elysées is jam-packed with eight lines of traffic stretching in both directions. The best time to stroll along this 'Avenue of the Elysian Fields' is thus in the very early morning, long before the city goes to work.

The avenue was laid out by the famous landscape architect Le Nôtre. At that time it served as an extension of the straight avenue which led from the Jardin des Tuileries through an area of swampland and then on to the heights of Chaillot. In 1670 this *Grand Cours* was opened as a promenade for coaches as far as the Rond-Point. The section further to the west remained neglected and uninhabited for a long time, though it was still used now and then for military exercises. It was only during the Second Empire that the Champs-Elysées was finally lined with buildings, and it soon became a very fashionable promenade. Since the end of World War II it has lost its former image of being the meeting-place of *tout Paris*, though whenever large demonstrations and parades are held – including the big 14 July parade – it becomes the focal point not just of Paris but of all France. Despite its impressive width (71m/230ft), the Champs-Elysées is still narrower than the Avenue Foch (120m/390ft). The shopping arcades here, built during recent years, contain boutiques, restaurants, ice-cream parlours, cinemas and luxury shops, all on various different levels. The famous Lido variety theatre used to be at No 76 until it moved to a former cinema. Despite the large number of coffee-houses both old and new, the place can no longer boast a genuine Parisian atmosphere.

Between the Place de la Concorde and the Avenue Franklin D. Roosevelt are the Grand Palais and the Petit Palais. These, along with the Pont Alexandre, were built on the occasion of the 1900 international exhibition in Neo-baroque, Belle Epoque style.

The 122-m (400-ft) facade of the ★ **Petit Palais** ⓭, with its rococo-style architecture, is distinctive for its monumental entrance that extends as far as the dome above. The sculptures on either side represent *The Seine and Her Tributaries* (left) and *The Four Seasons* (right). Since 1902 the Petit Palais has housed the Municipal Art Collection, the Musée des Beaux-Arts de la Ville de Paris. Among the most important works in the collection of paintings here are *Portrait of a Woman* by Lucas Cranach and a self-portrait by Rembrandt.

On the corner of the Avenue des Champs-Elysées stands a monument to statesman Georges Clémenceau (1841–1929). On the other side of the Avenue Winston Churchill is the ★ **Grand Palais** ⓮. In contrast to the attractive architecture of the Petit Palais, in many ways reminiscent of the 18th century, the Grand Palais marks a return to the heavier style of the 17th century.

The Grand Palais with its 5,000sq m (5,980sq yds) of space is an important exhibition centre, and hosts not only several art exhibitions but also the Paris Motor Show every

33

The Petit Palais

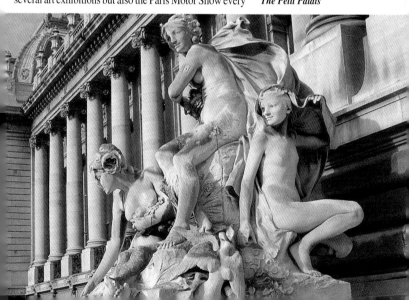

Arc de Triomphe

Guarding the Elysée Palace

spring. The west wing of the Palais de la Découverte contains a museum devoted to the progress of science and discovery (there is also a planetarium).

Via the Avenue de Marigny one then reaches the **Elysée Palace** ⓯ (65 Rue du Faubourg St-Honoré), the official seat of the president of France since 1873 (closed to the public). The Palais was built in 1722 by Claude Mollet, and Madame de Pompadour acquired it in 1753. Foreign ambassadors resided there during the reign of Louis XV; during the Revolution it was turned into a public ballroom. In 1806 it was presented to Napoleon's sister Caroline. After Waterloo, Napoleon signed his second abdication declaration here. Louis Napoleon Bonaparte lived in the palace as president of the Republic before moving to the Tuileries on 2 December 1851 as Napoleon III.

At the far end of the Champs-Elysées is the ★★**Arc de Triomphe** ⓰. In 1806, after the Battle of the Three Emperors at Austerlitz, Napoleon ordered the construction of a triumphal arch in honour of his glorious armies and to commemorate his victories. The architect he chose was Jean-François Chalgrin (1739–1811), who had the idea of shifting the triumphal arch planned for the Place de la Bastille to the end of the Champs-Elysées. Construction work on the mighty arch took a long time to complete. When Napoleon married Marie-Louise in 1810, only the foundations had been laid. Then work tailed off after the fall of Napoleon and the return of the Bourbons. It was only with the advent of Louis-Philippe (1836) that work on the arch was brought to completion.

During the Second Empire, the Place de l'Etoile and all the streets radiating from it were redesigned by Haussmann and Hittorf. George Haussmann (1809–91) was appointed prefect of the Seine in 1853 by Napoleon III and began the great task of improving Paris. He built bridges and laid out parks as well as redesigning the boulevards.

In 1840 Napoleon's mortal remains were brought home through the completed Arc de Triomphe, and in 1885 the hearse bearing Victor Hugo's coffin stood beneath the arch for a full two days. The Arc de Triomphe was – and still remains – the epitome of French *grandeur*. In 1921 an unknown French soldier, symbolising the 1,390,000 who fell during World War I, was laid to rest beneath the arch. The *Tombeau du Soldat Inconnu* (Tomb of the Unknown Soldier) was the first memorial of its type in the world.

The Arc de Triomphe is reached via a tunnel from the Avenue des Champs-Elysées. The arch contains a lot of sculpted decoration which softens the effect of the whole. The colossal statues on the main facades glorify the insurrection of 1792 and Napoleon's victories. The diagram shows where the various different sculptures are located.

ARC DE TRIOMPHE

East and South side

West and North side

A: *The Departure of the Volunteers of 1792,* also known as *La Marseillaise*, by François Rude, which is artistically the most interesting of the reliefs.
B: *Napoleon's Triumph after the Peace of 1810*, by J-P Cortot.
C: *The Burial of General Marceau, 1796*, by P H Lamaire.
D: *The Battle of Aboukir, 1799*, by B G Seurre.
E: *The Battle of Jemappes 1792*, by Marochetti.
F: *The Resistance of 1814*, by A Etex.
G: *The Peace of 1815*, also by A Etex.
H: *Crossing the Bridge of Arcole, 1796*, by J J Feuchère.
I: *The Capture of Alexandria, 1798*, by J E Chaponnière.
J: *The Battle of Austerlitz, 1805*, by Gechter and Chaillot.

Winged victories

The winged victories in the spandrels (ie the triangular areas between the arches) are the work of Jean-Jacques Pradier. The entire upper section of the structure is taken up by a frieze, with its 2-m (6.5-ft) high statues portraying the departure and glorious return of the *Grande Armée*. On the ledge above, round bucklers bear the names of Napoleon's battles, and the inside of the arch shows the names of 558 generals. The platform above the arch can be reached via a lift, and it provides one of the finest views of Paris (daily except public holidays, 10am–5pm, and until 6pm in summer).

Triumphal view

Elegant statuary

Sainte-Marie-Madeleine

Route 4

★ **Madeleine** – ★★ **Opéra** – ★★ **Palais-Royal** – ★★ **Place Vendôme** (Métro Concorde, lines 1, 8 and 12; bus Nos 24, 42, 52, 73, 84, 94)

This route provides a pleasant mixture of sightseeing and window-shopping in one of the most elegant shopping areas of the city.

It starts at the Métro station Concorde, with a stroll along the elegant Rue Royale in the direction of the Madeleine. At the end the street opens out into the Place de la Madeleine, with the Church of ★ **Sainte-Marie-Madeleine** ⓱ at its centre. A small church stood on this site in medieval times. Then in 1764, Louis XV laid the foundation-stone for the present structure at the end of the Rue Royale, placed there by the city planners as a *point de vue*. The first construction phase was based on plans by Constant d'Ivry, who wanted to model it after the Panthéon (*see page 57*). The building work was to take more than 80 years. In 1805 Napoleon decided to turn the half-finished church into a Temple of Glory for his *Grande Armée* following plans by architect Pierre Vignon. In 1808 the present-day structure assumed its Roman temple appearance. Construction work stopped on the building after the fall of Napoleon, and it was only finally consecrated in 1842.

The *cella* (interior of a classical temple) is bare and uninviting. The long hall is vaulted by three domes. The apse contains a romantic neoclassical fresco, showing Christ, Sainte-Madeleine and several historical figures including Napoleon.

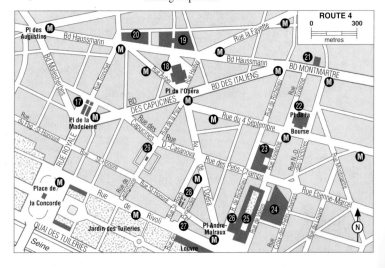

A flower market is held around this church from Tuesday to Friday. It was Baron Haussmann who gave the Place de la Madeleine its present-day appearance.

The route now continues along the Boulevard de la Madeleine and its extension, the Boulevard des Capucines (the composer Jacques Offenbach died at house No 8 in 1880). There is always a lot of brisk activity, especially in the afternoons, on the **Place de l'Opéra**, with its elegant shops and its famous Café de la Paix. This broad square was another brainchild of the Prefect Haussmann. The Café de la Paix was one of the city's most well-known meeting-points for politicians and literati during the Belle Epoque. It's still very pleasant even today to drink an apéritif at one of the small bistro tables here and watch the traffic rush by outside.

It's a dog's life

★★ **Opéra** . The city's opera house was built for the Académie Nationale de Musique et de Danse – the Paris Opera's official name – between 1862 and 1875, on the orders of Napoleon III, and cost a total of 48 million French francs. The architect, Charles Garnier, was unknown before he built it, and with this Opera House he successfully created the finest structure of the Second Empire. Alongside its main function as a venue for opera, the building had a second, social function too: the city's influential upper classes used to meet regularly in the foyer and in the square outside. This lavishly decorated building was equipped with entrance pavilions at the sides of the main facade, which simultaneously serve as *points de vue* from the boulevards leading up to them.

37

The main facade is composed of a series of arcades at ground level and the high colonnades of the main storey, and towering above them, the magnificent, crown-like dome of the auditorium and the huge tympanum above the stage area. Enormous sculptured groups adorn the front and corners of the facade, the highest of which shows Apollo with his lyre. The facade is richly embellished with artistic motifs. The medallions higher up contain the likenesses of famous composers, and the seven gilded bronze busts between the high twin columns of the loggia also represent composers.

The Opéra facade

The Pavillon d'Honneur on the left-hand side, with its double ramp, used to be the emperor's entrance. The president and guests of honour are still driven up to it today. The imperial recreation rooms beyond contain the Opera Library and also the Musée du Théâtre National de l'Opéra (daily, 11am–5pm).

Bust of Charles Garnier, the architect

The vestibule contains marble statues of the composers Lully, Rameau, Gluck and Handel. Beyond them are covered walks, halls of mirrors, foyers and further entrance halls, all of them confusingly elaborate. The large stairway (Escalier d'Honneur) leads from the entrance floor to

Galeries Lafayette

Musée Grevin

*Street
dramatics*

the level of the first balcony and covers the entire width of the auditorium.

A further architectural highlight is the Grand Foyer: its walls and vaulted ceilings are completely covered with paintings and sculptures. The five-storey horseshoe auditorium, decorated in Italian style, contains nearly 2,000 seats, though 258 of them do provide only a somewhat limited view of the stage. Since the opening of the Bastille Opera (*see page 80*) the building is now only used for ballet performances.

The intense colours of the ceiling, painted by Marc Chagall in 1964, blend harmoniously with the red and gold of the interior (daily, 10am–5pm).

Behind the Opera House on the Boulevard Haussmann is the large complex containing the **Galeries Lafayette** department store **19**. Though its exterior has undergone several alterations, this famous store's interior contains a 23-m (75-ft) high art nouveau central hall (1904–6 by G Chédanne) with multi-storey galleries, wrought-iron foliage decoration as well as an enormous dome made of coloured glass, all of which makes a brief stroll through here highly worthwhile.

Next door to it is the **Printemps** department store **20**, with its attractive gold and green mosaic facade. All that remains of its former interior layout is the colourful glass cupola above the self-service restaurant on its upper floor.

Other old department stores in Paris are the Samaritaine and Belle Jardinière, both on the Quai du Louvre, and also the Trois Quartiers on the Boulevard de la Madeleine.

Situated at No 10 Boulevard de Montmartre is the **Musée Grevin 21**, a wax museum containing effigies of contemporary personalities as well as historic scenes.

By heading south down the Rue Vivienne one arrives at the Place de la Bourse and the **Bourse 22**, or Stock Exchange, itself one of the most distinctive buildings of the Napoleonic era. With this representative structure Napoleon wanted to give visible expression to the social changes of his time.

An extension of the Rue Vivienne is the Rue Richelieu, and at No 58 is the **Bibliothèque Nationale 23**, which is the largest and most important library in all France, covering nearly 16,500sq m (19,700sq yds). The oldest section is the Hôtel Tubeuf, built in 1634, and taken over by Cardinal Mazarin in 1643. The building's eventual conversion into a library in the 19th century was supervised by Henri Labrouste. He was the first important architect in France to work with iron, and he equipped the reading-room – opened in 1868 – with a roof composed of nine iron cupolae.

The library today contains roughly 12 million books, 15 million engravings and photos, 180,000 manuscripts and a good half-million magazines (with around 30,000 works added annually). The library dates back to the Bibliothèque Royale of Charles V (1364–80). Louis XII then acquired the libraries of the Milanese Sforza family and also of the Gruuthuse family from Bruges. Francis I (1515–47) moved the collection to Fontainebleau and also stipulated that one copy of every work published in France should be delivered to the library free of charge – a regulation that still applies to this day. Henry IV had the collection moved back to Paris, to a former Jesuit monastery. In 1720, during the reign of Louis XV, the library was moved to its present-day location.

Worth a visit because of their various exhibitions are the Galerie Mansart and the large vestibule. One should take at least a brief look inside the hall beyond it, the Salle de Travail, although admission is only possible with a reading card. In the Salle d'Honneur (the administrative headquarters of the National Library) stands the model for the famous seated statue of Voltaire in old age, by Jean-Antoine Houdon, which is in the Comédie Française (daily Monday to Friday 9am–8pm, Saturday 9am–5.30pm).

On the Rue de Valois (reached from the National Library via the Rue des Petits Champs) lies the **Banque de France** ㉔. The oldest part of this whole complex is the Palais des Ducs de la Vrillière, built by F Mansart between 1635 and 1638. In 1719 the building was restored and became the Hôtel de Toulouse, the home of the Count of Toulouse, a son of King Louis XIV and Madame de Montespan. During the Revolution the national printing works were housed here; since 1811 it has been the headquarters of the Banque de France.

39

Banque de France

On the other side of the Rue de Valois there are several ways through to the **garden** of the **Palais-Royal**, a real oasis of tranquillity in the midst of all the big-city bustle. It was not always so peaceful, however. This garden used to be a meeting-point for agitators during the French Revolution: two days before the storming of the Bastille, the journalist Desmoulins issued his call to arms to the citizens here. It was from a trader in the Palais-Royal in 1793 that Charlotte Corday bought the knife with which she stabbed Marat in his bath. Jean Cocteau lived for years in an apartment in the Galerie Montpensier. Colette, one of the most Parisian of novelists, died in the Galerie Beaujolais (No 94) in 1954.

The northwestern corner of the Palais-Royal (17 Rue de Beaujolais) houses the restaurant **Grand Véfour**, considered to be one of the finest in Paris. Its decor is original and dates back to the time of the Directory (1795). Formerly called the Café de Chartres, this was a meeting place for some of the most important protagonists of the French Revolution.

The Grand Véfour

The oldest part of the ★★ **Palais-Royal** ❷ is not open to the public, because the *Conseil d'Etat* (State Council) holds its meetings there. Its job is to verify the constitutional correctness of all laws and regulations. The building also houses the Ministry of Culture.

Cardinal Richelieu, appointed prime minister in 1624, commissioned the architect Jacques Lemercier to build this *hôtel* near the Louvre. A few years later, after the adjacent city wall had been pulled down, the cardinal had the building converted into a large residence (1634–9). The Corps de Logis was framed by outbuildings on both the front and rear. Before his death in 1642, the cardinal appointed King Louis XIII his successor. From then on, only the king himself or the crown prince (dauphin) were allowed to live in the Palais Cardinal.

Then the brother of King Louis XIV, Philippe d'Orléans, moved in with his son of the same name. The latter gave the building its present-day appearance, and held wild parties there.

Cool ices on offer

Joseph d'Orléans, the father of later 'Citizen King' Louis-Philippe, also lived here from 1776; as Philippe-Egalité he voted in favour of Louis XVI's execution, before being executed himself in 1793. He had the garden behind the palace surrounded by a series of long galleries containing shops. After the revolution this complex with its restaurants and casinos became the focal point of Parisian life, until the Palais fell to the Orléans once again after the fall of Napoleon. During the Paris Commune (1871) the Palais-Royal burnt down, but was then faithfully reconstructed by Chabrol (1872–6). The galleries still contain several second-hand bookshops, philately shops and restaurants.

Next to the Palais-Royal is the **Théâtre Français** ❷. Its entrance is in the Place André Malraux on the Rue de Richelieu. On the eastern side of the square is the monument to poet Alfred de Musset (1810–75). The Duke of Orléans, Philippe-Egalité, had this theatre constructed according to plans by Victor Louis (1786–90), and it was given its present-day facade by Prosper Chabrol in 1867. Since 1799 this building has been the headquarters of the Comédie Française, formed in 1680 when several smaller theatre groups merged with Molière's ensemble. Less than a year later, Louis XIV designated the building his court theatre, and Napoleon Bonaparte made it his state theatre. The productions staged here today are mostly taken from the classical repertoire.

Medallion of Molière

On the entrance facade facing the Rue de Richelieu, medallions showing Corneille, Molière, Racine and Victor Hugo can be seen. The foyer and the stairwell are decorated with busts and monuments to famous actors and poets. The foyer also contains the chair in which Molière

was sitting in 1673 during a performance of *Le Malade imaginaire* when he collapsed. He died shortly afterwards. The original of the famous statue of Voltaire seated (*see page 39*) can also be admired here.

Statue of Joan of Arc

41

According to the plans drawn up by Paris Prefect Baron Haussmann, work began on constructing the Avenue de L'Opéra in order to connect Place de l'Opéra and Place André-Malraux. During the construction work the Colline St-Roch, between the Rue Thérèse and the Rue des Pyramides, had to be removed. Joan of Arc had once used it as a cannon emplacement while fighting the English.

The route continues along the Rue de Rivoli in the direction of the Place de la Concorde. In the middle of the small **Place des Pyramides** ㉗ stands the **golden equestrian statue of Joan of Arc**. It was placed on the site where, according to legend, the Maid of Orléans was wounded in 1429 during the Paris siege. There is a procession to this statue on All Saints' Day every year.

In the Rue St-Honoré, at No 296, is the Church of **Saint-Roch** ㉘, standing in the centre of the Quartier St-Honoré. Louis XIV laid the foundation-stone for this church in 1653, and the building was consecrated to the patron saint of plague victims, St-Roch. The building was designed by Jacques Lemercier. Construction work had to be brought to a halt in 1600, though, due to lack of funds, and it was only recommenced in 1701, according to an altered plan by Hardouin-Mansart. The facade – based on a design by Robert de Cotte – was finally completed between 1736 and 1740.

Church of St-Roch

This large parish church – 126m (410ft) long – is distinctive above all for the effective use of space in its choir section – a result of the additions made during its two phases of construction. Hardouin-Mansart extended the choir by adding the oval St Mary's Chapel, and the small Communion Chapel was added a few years later. Between

1754 and 1760, as a final extension of the choir axis, the Calvary Chapel was built; inside, a marble crucifix, dramatically lit, appears above Mt Calvary.

St-Roch was once the most magnificent baroque church in all Paris, but most of the fine sculpture it contained was lost during the revolution, as were the statues on its elegant facade (the present-day ones date from the 19th century). Nevertheless the church does still have a rich collection of excellent 17th-century religious works of art, brought there in 1819 from demolished Paris churches.

On 5 October 1795 several rebellious royalists who had barricaded themselves into the church were summarily shot on the church steps on the orders of Napoleon Bonaparte. Bullet-holes and other traces from the battle can be seen on the church wall.

The Rue St-Honoré and a right turn into the Rue Castiglione lead on to the ★★ **Place Vendôme** ㉙, the architectural heart of the distinguished Faubourg St-Honoré, and one of the most elegant squares in Paris. Its construction dates back to the reign of Louis XIV and his architect Jules Hardouin-Mansart.

According to the original plans, today's Place Vendôme was to have been a royal square with a statue of the king at its centre, surrounded by public buildings. Construction work began on the facades in 1687, but no buyers could be found for the strips of land behind them. The completion of the square – which was initially known as Place Louis-le-Grand – thus dragged on until 1720.

Triumphal Column detail, Place Vendôme

The history of the monument in the middle closely reflects French history. In 1792, during the revolution, the equestrian statue of the king, placed there in 1699, was destroyed, and Napoleon then had the 43-m (140-ft) high **Triumphal Column** (Colonne de la Grande Armée) placed there (1806–10) and decorated with reliefs commemorating the glorious campaigns of the imperial army. The bronze used to make the statue was taken from 1,200 pieces of enemy cannon captured during the various battles. A statue of Napoleon stood at the top of the column, but Napoleon III found it too small and had it replaced by the Roman-style imperial one up there today. In 1871 the column was pulled down by Communard insurrectionists. Since the painter Gustave Courbet was suspected of having had a hand in the deed, he paid for the monument's re-erection out of his own pocket.

Window shopping

The Place de Vendôme has survived revolution and insurrection with remarkably litle damage. Today it is the home of wealthy bankers and exclusive jewellers, of which Cartier is probably the best known. The Ministry of Justice is situated at Nos 11–13. The composer Frédéric Chopin died at No 12 in 1849. At No 15 stands the elegant Ritz Hotel, established at the turn of the century.

Route 5

★★ Forum des Halles – ★★★ Centre Pompidou – ★ Hotel de Ville (*Métro Les Halles, line 4; bus Nos 29, 74, 85*)

On the Place des Deux-Ecus stands the round building housing the **Bourse du Commerce ㉚**. Today's Commercial Exchange stands on the site of a former *palais* belonging to Cathérine de Médicis that was demolished in 1748. The 31-m (100-ft) high column on the south side still dates from this earlier structure, and is thought to have been used for astronomical observation (a spiral staircase used to lead up to the platform from inside the building). In 1767 a Grain Exchange was built on the site, a round building which was then replaced in 1889 by the present Bourse du Commerce. The huge glass-and-iron dome was retained.

Bourse du Commerce

Not far away, on the edge of the Forum des Halles (1 Rue du Jour), lies the Church of **★★ Saint-Eustache ㉛**. Work started on this church in 1532 after a generous grant from Francis I, and it became Paris' first ever Renaissance building. Its interior is distinctive for the way it combines an architectural background that is purely Gothic with an imaginative experimentation with Italian Renaissance motifs that is unique in France.

Saint-Eustache

43

The original plans were very ambitious. They show a complex with ground-plan and dimensions (106m/350ft long, 34m/110ft high) rivalling those of Notre-Dame, with five aisles, ambulatory and chevet.

The broad windows reveal simplified tracery that is ribbon-like and devoid of tension. The Gothic pointed arch has been replaced by a more rounded version. The stained-

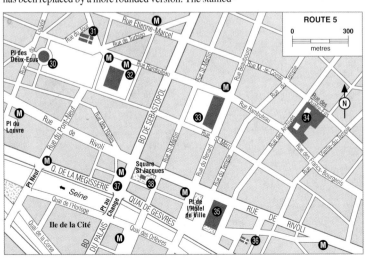

Saint-Eustache, interior

glass windows in the choir are all that remain of the original ones. The interior is flooded with light, the atmosphere is joyful. 'Notre-Dame updated.'

Despite the length of time it took to build (well over 100 years), Saint-Eustache was finally completed according to the original plans of an unknown architect. The impression the church makes as a whole is spoilt only by its facade – a rather boring late 18th-century copy of the facade of St-Sulpice.

The parish of Saint-Eustache included not only the numerous merchants in the Halles district but also those members of the nobility who owned *hôtels* in the direction of the Louvre. The church thus contains the tombs of several famous people, including that of Colbert, Louis XIV's powerful finance minister. A funeral ceremony was also held in Saint-Eustache for Mozart's mother when she died during a stay in Paris. Molière, Cardinal Richelieu and Jeanne Poisson (later Madame de Pompadour) were all christened in the church. Louis XIV received his first communion here, in 1649.

The interior was badly damaged by fire in 1844, but has been carefully restored. During the restoration work, frescoes dating from the 17th century were discovered in some of the chapels in the ambulatory.

Intimate bistro eating
Fun fair at Les Halles

The restaurants and bistros in the area surrounding the ★★ **Forum des Halles** ㉜ can still serve you onion soup, snails and oysters, but this part of Paris has definitely lost its former flair. The area where the famous old iron-and-glass market halls used to stand until 1972 is now occupied by a four-storey shopping centre with restaurants, cinemas, a theatre, a holographic museum as well as a wax museum (Nouveau Musée Grevin) containing Parisian scenes from the last century. Another enormous shopping arcade leads off in the direction of the Bourse du

Commerce, with a huge glass-house full of exotic plants. Alongside sports facilities (including an indoor swimming-pool) there are also various cultural and entertainment facilities (photo gallery, cinemas, discotheque). And beneath it all is the largest underground station in Europe, containing the lines of the RER (Réseau Express Régional) and the Métro, as well as several multi-storey car-parks.

We now come to the ★★★ **Centre National d'Art et de Culture** ❸❸ in Rue du Renaud, usually known as the **Centre Pompidou** or **Centre Beaubourg** (Monday, Wednesday, Thursday, Friday 12noon–10pm, Saturday, Sunday 10am–10pm; closed Tuesday, also 1 May, 25 December). This construction, created between 1972 and 1977 by the architects Richard Rogers, Renzo Piano and Gianfranco Franchini at the request of ex-president Pompidou, has radically altered the *quartier* of Beaubourg. It has provided Paris with a new landmark which – though highly controversial initially – has grown into one of the most popular tourist destinations in the city.

Centre Pompidou

The building, made entirely of glass and surrounded by a white steel grid, looks most unusual because its services and structure have been exposed externally and painted in primary colours. The five floors are supported by steel beams set into external scaffolding made up of 84 steel girders, each one weighing 73 tons. The centre also houses the **Musée National d'Art Moderne** (on the 3rd and 4th floors) including works by Picasso, Braque and Matisse, a huge library (taking up at least three floors), and a cinema as well as the Institute of Acoustic and Musical Research (IRCAM).

45

The square in front of the Centre Pompidou provides the best view of the mammoth digital clock, counting away the remaining seconds until the year 2000.

Housed in the former Hôtel de Soubise at 60 Rue des Francs-Bourgeois are the **Archives Nationales** ❸❹, the largest national archives in the world. François de Rohan, Prince of Soubise, purchased the Hôtel de Clisson with the money he received from Louis XIV after having allowed His Majesty to spend several happy hours with his attractive wife. Conversion of the *hôtel* was entrusted to a Mansart pupil unknown until that time, Pierre-Alexis Delamair. Of the original building, only the main portal remains. The generously-proportioned three-winged structure with its colonnades today surrounds the spacious courtyard. The magnificent interior should definitely be visited. The high point of any visit is the oval salon, an absolute masterpiece of the rococo style (daily 2pm–5pm except Tuesday).

Rococo in the Archives Nationales

The **Place de l'Hôtel de Ville** used to be known as the Place de Grève (*grève* means beach), and was used for the loading and unloading of Seine shipping during the Mid-

Hôtel de Ville

dle Ages. From 1310 until 1830 the Place de Grève was used for public executions, and was also where the city's unemployed would hold their meetings. The French term for 'to go on strike' is still *faire le grève*.

Dominating the square is the ★ **Hôtel de Ville** ㉟. The city council under Etienne Marcel first occupied the Maison aux Pilliers on the Place de Grève. Under Francis I the city's largely dilapidated first town hall was replaced by a second one, built in 1533 by the Italian Domenico da Cortana (known as Bocador), who had already made a name for himself designing the Loire châteaux at Chambord and Blois. The building was only finally completed in 1628 because of the Wars of Religion. During the 1871 Paris Commune it was destroyed by fire but was reconstructed in its original form in 1873–82.

Bocador's design for the facade with its miniscule decoration is typical of the early application of Italian Renaissance motifs to buildings that were still essentially Gothic, with high pointed windows and steep roofs.

The city goddess of Paris sits high up on the clock tower, overlooking the pedestrianised square, and below are the Herculean figures representing Work and Activity, by Hiolle (late 19th-century). The garden on the south side contains an equestrian statue of Etienne Marcel.

The staterooms and banqueting rooms are fine examples of the theatrical Belle Epoque style that was so popular at the end of the 19th century. The stairway known as the Escalier d'Honneur is particularly noteworthy, with the painted ceiling (1891) by Puvis de Chavannes.

The Hôtel de Ville houses the offices of the city's mayor and is the headquarters of the municipal administration. Official banquets and state receptions for visiting VIPs are held here, when the Salle des Fêtes, with its glittering crystal chandeliers, really comes into its own.

Lamp-post detail, Place de l'Hôtel de Ville

To the east of the Hôtel de Ville lies the Church of **St-Gervais-St-Protais** ㊱. Work began on its construction in 1494, but lasted right up to the beginning of the 17th century. The facade, built between 1616 and 1617, was something utterly new at the time. Though Salomon de Brossé modelled it on the Roman baroque facade, its three storeys of double pillars lend it a particular severity. Because of its sparseness of detail it is considered to be one of the earliest examples of French Classicism. The interior is still predominantly Late Gothic.

St-Gervais-St-Protais

The interior is a three-aisled basilica with side-chapels. The central nave is surmounted by a star-ribbed vault, and the transept contains Renaissance balconies. Only a few of the original stained-glass windows still remain. The finest are the one in the southern choir chapel, showing the Judgement of Solomon (1531), and the one in the chapel next door showing St-Gervais and St-Protais.

To the west of the Hôtel de Ville, before the Pont au Change (Moneychangers' Bridge), lies the **Place du Châtelet** ㊲. The name commemorates the bulwark known as the Grand Châtelet that was set up at the head of the bridge in 1130 for monitoring pedestrian traffic over the river to the Ile de la Cité. Deprived of its function in 1109, when Philippe II Augustus built the city wall, the Châtelet then became the official residence of the Provost of Paris, appointed by the king to keep an eye on law and order, and remained so until the function was abolished in 1790 as a result of the revolution. The fortress used to contain the city guard, the law courts, torture chambers and dungeons. During the reign of Napoleon the gloomy old building was torn down, and the emperor had a victory column built on the open square thus created. Haussmann gave the square its present-day appearance. The column was placed on a plinth inside the rounded basin of the Fontaine du Châtelet. In 1800 the theatre buildings opposite were built by Davioud: the Théâtre du Châtelet, which seats 3,600 (it was the most important theatre in the city until the construction of the Opera House), and the Théâtre Sarah-Bernhardt.

47

Column detail,
Place du Châtelet
Fontaine du Châtelet

Northeast of the square is the Square St-Jacques with the **Tour St-Jacques** ㊳. This tower, built between 1508 and 1522, is all that remains of the parish church that was once the spiritual centre of the densely populated Châtelet *quartier*. Both the church and the Rue St-Jacques, which runs through the Latin Quarter on the opposite bank of the Seine, are named after St James, reminders that they lay on the route travelled by medieval pilgrims coming from the north and heading for Santiago de Compostela in Spain, to visit the tomb of the saint.

The top of the tower is a fine example of the richness and complexity of Late Gothic decoration.

Route 6

Plaque with plan of the Bastille

PLAN DE LA BASTILLE COMMENCÉE EN 1370
PRISE PAR LE PEUPLE LE 14 JUILLET 1789
ET DÉMOLIE LA MÊME ANNÉE.

LE PÉRIMÈTRE DE LA FORTERESSE
EST TRACÉ SUR LE SOL DE CETTE PLACE
14 JUILLET 1880.

★★ **Place de la Bastille** ❸❾. The bulwark erected during the reign of Charles V (1364–80) to protect his nearby residence (the Hôtel St-Pol) once used to stand on this square, and Parisians called it *la petite Bastille* (the little bastion). It was supposed to allow the king to flee to safety through the nearby Porte St-Antoine to Vincennes in the event of any trouble. Unfortunately, the fortress's military role was only slight; it withstood just one of seven sieges during the civil wars.

Under Henry IV the state treasure was placed there. Richelieu finally had the fortress converted into a prison, and Voltaire, Mirabeau and the Marquis de Sade were just a few of its prominent inmates. On 14 July 1789, the storming of the Bastille marked the start of the French Revolution. At first the mob only surrounded it because they assumed the building contained arms and ammunition. When several hours of negotiations between the rebels and

48

the commander failed to produce any result, the prison was stormed, and the commander was beheaded along with nine of his soldiers. When the keys were finally found, the Bastille's seven remaining prisoners – four counterfeiters, two madmen, and a young aristocrat who had displeased his father – were liberated. Fourteenth of July has been a French national holiday since 1790. The demolition of the Bastille began the next day. The ground plan of the original building is marked in light-coloured stones on the western side of the square, in the Rue St-Antoine.

Opéra de la Bastille

On the eastern side of the square stands the **Opéra de la Bastille**, opened in 1989. This modern building by Carlos Ott was opened on the 200-year anniversary of the French Revolution. The Grande Salle has room for 2,700 spectators. The amphitheatre and an experimental stage (still under construction) can be seen from the foyer.

At the centre of the Place de la Bastille is the **Colonne de Juillet**, erected in 1840. This 47-m (150-ft) high victory column, made of bronze in the shape of a huge tombstone, commemorates the victims of the July Revolution of 1830 who are buried beneath it.

Colonne de Juillet

★★ **Place des Vosges** ⓸. The royal Hôtel des Tournelles – where King Henry II met his end in a tournament in 1559 – used to stand in the middle of this square, and formed the centre point of the Marais quarter. The king's widow, Cathérine de Médicis, considered building a square once the *hôtel* had been demolished, but the idea was only implemented during the reign of Henry IV. The closed square, each side measuring 108m (350ft), is surrounded by 36 facades forming a harmonious whole. The most distinctive feature is the way the facades have been designed, with their mixture of ground-floor arcades, *porte-fenêtres*, and high dormer windows.

Place des Vosges   **49**

In 1612 the square was named La Place and during the revolution that it was renamed the Place des Vosges. In 1639 Richelieu had the equestrian statue of Louis XIII placed in the centre of the square. After the revolution, the original was so badly damaged that it had to be replaced by a copy. From 1832 to 1848, Victor Hugo lived on the second floor of house No 6. In honour of the poet's hundredth birthday (1902) the city of Paris installed the **Musée Victor Hugo** ⓺ there (daily 10am–5.40pm except Monday and public holidays). Covering two floors are over 400 sketches by Hugo, as well as his study and writing desk, his death-mask and his deathbed.

Victor Hugo

In the Rue de Sévigné, at No 23, lies the ★ **Hôtel Carnavalet** ⓻. The architect behind this Renaissance building, built between 1544 and 1550, is thought to have been Pierre Lescot, who probably worked with the sculptor Jean Goujon here just as he had on the Louvre. The building's present name comes from the distortion of the name of one

Louis XIV as Roman emperor

Hôtel Carnavalet, exterior

of its former owners, Françoise de Kernevenoy, altered by the Parisians to Carnavalet. Madame de Sévigné, writer of witty letters and chronicler of life at the court of the Sun King Louis XIV, lived in this house from 1677 until her death in 1696.

All that remains today of the original Renaissance building are the portal on the street and the oft-restored façade of the Corps de Logis in the Cour d'Honneur (Courtyard of Honour). The courtyard contains the only **statue** of the Sun King to have survived the revolution; it portrays Louis XIV as a Roman emperor.

This *hôtel* has housed the **Museum of Municipal History** since 1880 (the museum was extended in 1989 with the addition of the Hôtel Le Peletier de Saint-Fargeau, in the same street). The important collection here documents the history of Paris from its very beginning until the present (daily except Monday, 10am–5.40pm).

Next comes the ★★★ **Musée Picasso/Hôtel Salé 43**, 5 Rue de Thorigny (daily except Tuesday 9.15am–5.15pm, Wednesday until 10pm). This *hôtel* (the name *salé* derives from the salt tax its former owner used to levy) was built in the mid-17th century. The Picasso Museum was moved here in 1985. Thanks to a donation by the heirs of the great Spanish painter, the French state possesses 200 paintings and over 300 sketches and etchings, along with numerous sculptures, ceramics, collages and reliefs. All of Picasso's artistic phases are clearly documented here, and 50 works from his private collection (including Braque, Cézanne) are also on display.

Not far away, at the Hôtel Donon, 8 Rue Elzévir, is the **Musée Cognacq-Jay** (Tuesday to Sunday 10am–12.30pm and 1.45–5.45pm), moved here in 1991, with its collection of artworks from the century of the Enlightenment. The building (constructed during the second

Musée Picasso, interior

half of the 16th century) contains several painted roof-beams dating from shortly after its completion.

At No 10 in the Rue Pavée lies the **Synagogue** ❹❹ built by Hector Guimard, who also constructed the city's art nouveau Métro entrances. Recessed in the row of houses, the facade features the convex and concave style that is typically art nouveau. The interior, with its dynamic forms painted entirely in white, is extremely interesting.

The Jewish quarter of Paris, with its synagogues and workshops, and also several good kosher restaurants, is south of the Rue des Francs-Bourgeois in the area between the Rue du Bourg Tibourg, Rue du Roi de Sicilie, Rue Malher and the Rue des Rosiers.

A slower pace of life

In the Rue Vieille du Temple stands the ★★ **Hôtel de Rohan** ❹❺ (noon–6pm daily, except Monday and public holidays), which was built for the prince-bishop of Strasburg, Maximilian de Rohan, between 1704 and 1709. On the garden side there is a magnificent relief by Le Lorrain above the entrance to the former stables: *The Wild Sun-Horses of Apollo Drinking*. Inside, the Cabinet des Singes, with its magnificent rococo decoration (c 1750), is particularly fine.

In the Rue du Perche is the tiny Church of **St-Jean-St-François** ❹❻, which contains several important works, including Germain Pilon's statue, *St Francis in Ecstasy*.

In the Rue des Archives is the **Hôtel Guénégaud** ❹❼. Built in 1648–51, it is the only building in Paris that can be proved to be the work of the great architect François Mansart (1598–1666). The facade of the building – which today houses the Musée de la Chasse (Hunting Museum) – is noticeably restrained.

The most northerly of the sights on this route is the **Place de la République** ❹❽, with the monument to the republic at its centre. The bronze reliefs on the plinth portray the most important events in the history of the French Republic from 1789 to 1880. The lion with the urn represents universal suffrage. Numerous large boulevards and streets meet up at this square, which is 282m (925ft) long and 119m (390ft) wide.

51

Monument to the Republic, Place de la République

To the east of the square lies the poorest part of the city centre, crammed with dilapidated tenement blocks. Small craft businesses still exist in several of the rear courtyards, and many of the city's carpentry workshops are located here.

South of the square, at the Boulevard du Temple, is the **Cirque d'Hiver** ❹❾, a neoclassical edifice built in 1852 to a design by the Cologne architect Hittorf. The building has since been converted into a multi-purpose hall, and can accommodate up to 6,000 people. The famous Bouglione circus family has a long-term lease on the building, but numerous other events take place here too.

Cirque d'Hiver, home to the Bouglione circus

Souvenir window, Montmartre

Going underground

Route 7

★★ **Montmartre** (*Métro Place de Clichy, lines 2 and 13; bus Nos 30, 54, 68*)

In ancient times a temple lay on this hill, or butte, and was probably consecrated to the god Mercury (a chronicle of 742 refers to the hill as *mons mercore*). This early name gradually developed into Montmartre, the name for the highest hill in Paris (130m/425ft).

Montmartre is famed the world over as a place of entertainment. Nightclubs, bars and *Variétés* tend to be concentrated on its southern slope, however, between the Place Pigalle and the Place Blanche. Up on the hill itself, several quiet corners have retained the picturesque atmosphere of the area's earlier days as an artists' quarter, though much has been sacrificed to tourism.

The best place to start this route is at the Place de Clichy. Proceed along the Boulevard de Clichy in the direction of the Place Pigalle, with all its restaurants. It's hard to miss the **Moulin-Rouge** ⑩, with its big sails. It was a famous ballroom as long ago as the turn of the century. Toulouse-Lautrec captured the charm of the Moulin-Rouge in his paintings of the dancer La Goulue.

The real heart of the entertainment district is the ★ **Place Pigalle** ⑪. This square, with its huge striptease advertisements and billboards, is a known tourist trap, but as long as one is aware of that, it is worth seeing. It is also worth mentioning that the famous Impressionist painter Edgar Degas died at No 6 in 1917.

One street typical of the area is the Rue André-Antoine, which leads to the picturesque **Place des Abbesses** ⑫ with its old **Métro entrance** and the **Church of St-Jean-**

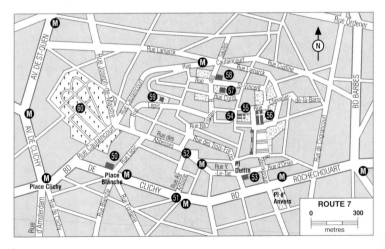

l'Evangéliste. The brick facade conceals the very first re-inforced concrete structure in all of Paris, completed in 1904. Further to the east, on the Place Charles-Dullin, lies the Théâtre de L'Atelier **53**. Jean-Louis Barrault had his first successes here.

The domes of Sacré Coeur Saint-Jean-l'Evangeliste

Place du Tertre 54 is the old village square of Montmartre, which used to be an independent municipality in its own right. The former town hall is on the south side of the square at No 5. During the day, artists both genuine and fake stand at their easels here attempting to sell their works to the tourists.

Impressions of the Place du Tertre

St-Pierre-de-Montmartre 55, one of the oldest churches in the city, is just a few steps away from the Place du Tertre. A Benedictine monastery was originally founded on this site by Louis VI in 1133, and was consecrated in 1147. Henry IV set up his headquarters here while Paris was under siege because the vantage point gave him a fine view of troop movements below. Towards the end of the 17th century, when a new monastery was built close to today's Place des Abbesses, the old building up on the Montmartre hill was finally demolished. St-Pierre still contains vestiges of an earlier Merovingian structure (double pillars in the triforium, capitals) as well as four marble pillars (at the entrance and in the choir) which most probably date from Roman times. North of the church lies the Cimetière St-Pierre, probably the oldest cemetery in Paris, but it is only open to the public on All Saints' Day (1 November).

Its fine situation at the highest point of the butte makes the ★★ **Sacré-Coeur 56** an international tourist attraction. Its foundation dates back to a vow taken by the Catholics of Paris to build a national church of expiation after the trauma of losing the war against Prussia in 1871. Construction work began in 1875, to designs by architect Paul Abadie.

It took almost 40 years to build Sacré-Coeur and when it was finished, in 1914, its consecration was delayed by the outbreak of World War I. It was finally consecrated as the Church of the Sacred Heart on 9 October 1919.

The Sacré-Coeur is a cruciform, centrally-planned building in the form of a square, with a high main dome and four smaller subsidiary domes. The equestrian statues on either side of the entrance, showing Saint-Louis and Joan of Arc, by Lefèbvre, were erected in 1927. The broad, high interior (110m/360ft long, 50m/160ft wide) is dominated by the enormous, Byzantine-style mosaic of Christ in the apse.

The view from Sacré-Coeur

The parvis affords one of the very best views of the entire city. The bronze entrance doors are sculpted with scenes from the life of Christ. The broad flight of steps in front has become a popular meeting-place for young people. Alongside this monumental terraced stairway there is also a funicular railway. Those not keen on climbing the steps can take a minibus from the Place Pigalle.

The painter Auguste Renoir used to have his studio at No 12 Rue Cortot. Suzanne Valadon, Maurice Utrillo (her son) and Raoul Dufy all painted there too. The building's former garden-house is now the **Musée du Vieux-Montmartre 57** (daily except Monday 11am–6pm; closed 1 January, 1 May and 25 December). This museum documents such figures from Montmartre's past as painter Emile Bernard and the famous mayor Clémenceau, and also contains exhibits from the cabarets and theatres of the Belle Epoque.

The corner formed by Rue des Saules and Rue St-Vincent is one of the most picturesque corners of today's Montmartre. The last few vines grow here, on a hill that once used to be covered with them. Every autumn, when the grapes are harvested, the vineyard here becomes the centre of a wine festival.

The Lapin Agile

Opposite is the picturesque inn known as the **Lapin Agile 58**, or Agile Rabbit. This establishment was once a meeting-place for Picasso, Utrillo and several other painters when they were still unknown. It owes its name to the painter A Gill, who painted his name and a rabbit on the inn-sign – nothing to do with agility.

On a small rise between the Avenue Junot and the Rue Lepic is the **Moulin de la Galette 59**. Renoir's masterpiece *Bal au Moulin de la Galette*, today in the Musée d'Orsay, made the Moulin and its garden world-famous when it was an inn and dance hall.

Several famous people lie buried in the **Cimetière Montmartre 60**, including composers Adolphe Adam, Jacques Offenbach and Hector Berlioz, writers Alexandre Dumas, Fils, Heinrich Heine, Stendhal and Théophile Gautier, actor Sacha Guitry and the singer Dalida.

Route 8

★★ Quartier Latin – ★★ Boulevard St-Germain (*Métro St-Michel. line 4; bus Nos 21, 24, 27, 38, 47, 85, 96*)

The Latin Quarter is the second-oldest part of Paris after the Ile de la Cité. The first university was founded here in the 12th century. Until the revolution, Latin was not only the language used for university lectures but was also spoken outside the academic environment. Today the Quartier Latin, full of schoolchildren and students, is still the intellectual centre of the city and intense debates are still held in the various clubs and societies. It was here that the student unrest of 1968 began.

Café in the Quartier Latin

The main traffic arteries in the Latin Quarter are the Boulevard St-Michel (also known familiarly as the Boul Mich) and the Boulevard St-Germain. The starting-point on this route is the **Place St-Michel**. The huge **Fontaine St-Michel** was designed by Davioud (1858–60). It shows St-Michel the dragon-slayer surrounded by four figures representing wisdom, justice, strength and moderation, respectively. The coat-of-arms of the city of Paris can be seen on the tympanum. Today this fountain is a popular rendezvous point.

Fontaine St-Michel

55

The Rue de la Harpe and the Rue St-Séverin lead to ★ **Saint-Séverin ⑥**, built in the Flamboyant style, and one of the finest Late Gothic churches in Paris. The building was begun in 1220 and extended in the 14th century, but much of it was destroyed in a bad fire at the begin-

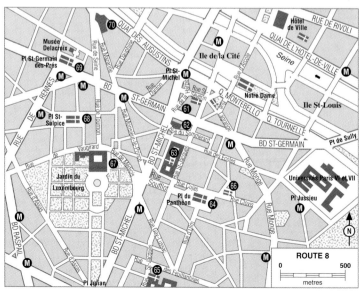

Interior, Saint-Séverin

In the Musée de Cluny

Berets never go out of fashion

ning of the 15th century. The five-aisled interior with its side-chapel extensions is unusually wide and bright, and the ambulatory, with its net vault, is particularly fine. The cemetery is surrounded by cloister-like ossuaries. The tracery on the rose window adorning the west front is typically Late Gothic.

In the Rue St-Julien stands ★ **St-Julien-le-Pauvre**. A chapel consecrated to St Julian the martyr stood here in the 6th century and the present church was built at the same time as Notre-Dame opposite, and until the 16th century was used as a congregation hall for Paris University. Today the city's Greek Orthodox community holds its services here. At the side of the church is the small Square Viviani, where there is a superb view of Notre-Dame.

A visit to the ★★ **Musée National du Moyen Age** (**Musée de Cluny**) ❷ (daily except Tuesday and public holidays 9.30am–5.50pm), housed in the former palais of the abbots of Cluny (Rue du Sommerard), is definitely worthwhile. The complex, with its three wings grouped around a central courtyard, is sealed off from the street by a wall. The building has been greatly altered through the years, and only the ★ chapel and a room with a quadripartite net vault roof survive.

The museum contains a large collection of medieval arts and crafts. On the first floor there are tapestries dating from the 15th and early 16th century, including the renowned six-panel unicorn tapestry *Dame à la Licorne*, perhaps the finest *Millefleur* tapestry here. The Salle Notre-Dame contains the heads that were knocked off the royal statues of Notre-Dame, representing the biblical kings of Judah. The ruins of the Roman ★ **thermal baths** (AD200) are also housed here.

On the Rue St-Jacques is the vast complex of the **Sorbonne** ❻. Today the largest university in France, it was

founded as a college in 1257 by Robert de Sorbon, chaplain to Louis IX, offering education and accommodation to needy theology students. The institute grew in size and reputation until its name was finally transferred to the University of Paris in the 19th century. Today's building last underwent alteration by the architect Nénot in 1901, when previous buildings constructed under Richelieu in 1642, such as the Cour d'Honneur and the university church of ★ **Ste-Ursule-de-la-Sorbonne**, had to be taken into consideration. The architect commissioned at that time was Lemercier, whose plans for the two-storeyed ★ main facade with its gables, pillars and enormous Jesuit-style dome were considered quite revolutionary.

The domed building at the end of the Rue Soufflot is the ★★ **Panthéon ④**. It stands on the small rise of the ancient Mons Luticius, consecrated to the patron saint of Paris, Ste-Geneviève (*see page 73*), in the Middle Ages. The abbey in her name stood here until the beginning of the 19th century, when it was pulled down, leaving just the tower and part of the refectory on the Rue Clotilde. The new building was commissioned by Louis XV as a votive offering after he recovered from a serious illness. In 1756 the foundation stone for the ambitious new building was laid slightly to the west of the old abbey. It was modelled on St Peter's in Rome. Architecturally, the exterior is worthy of particular note: the 117-m (380-ft) high dome is supported by a ring of pillars. The high and elegant domed interior – with a fresco by Gros (1815–24) portraying the deification of Ste-Geneviève – is filled with light. This clear and harmonious use of space makes the building the masterpiece of its architect, Jacques-Germain Soufflot, who died ten years before its completion.

The Panthéon

Almost immediately after the building was completed in 1791 the revolutionary authorities decided to make the church into a last resting place for heroes of the revolution. Voltaire's mortal remains were transferred to the Panthéon crypt that same year. He was followed not only by Jean-Jacques Rousseau and Victor Hugo, but also by the remains of the World War II Resistance leader Jean Moulin, for whom a symbolic tomb was built in the 1970s (daily except public holidays 10am–4pm).

Statue of Voltaire, Panthéon

At No 277 on the Rue St-Jacques stands the famous church of **Val-de-Grâce ⑤**. It was designed according to the plans of François Mansart. Anne of Austria had vowed to build the church if she bore a son, and after the safe birth of the future Louis XIV, Mansart was given the commission; his original plans were however altered by his successor on the scheme, Jacques Lemercier.

The building's facade is famous for the way it combines the mighty dome at the back with the appearance of the structure as a whole. Mansart's interior also has several

St-Etienne-du-Mont

Jardin du Luxembourg

recognisably Italian ideas: the nave and the central building form a unity, and the majestic dome room where the choir and the huge transepts meet up is an extension of the main hall. The colourful flooring is highly decorative, and its pattern harmonises with that of the barrel vault above. There is a large baldachin altar with barley-sugar columns beneath the dome. The monastery building contains a cloister, a school for army doctors and, attached to it, a medical museum.

Behind the Panthéon, in the Rue St-Etienne-du-Mont, lies the Church of ★ **St-Etienne-du-Mont** ❻❻. This used to be the parish church of the Abbey of Ste-Geneviève. Because of the increase in population in the city's university quarter, a new building was decided on in 1492. Construction work dragged on until 1622 with the result that this church – like St-Eustache and St-Gervais – is a mixture of several different styles. The facade – the last section to be completed – reveals a carefree interplay of Gothic and antique elements. Inside, there are Gothic pointed arches in the choir – the oldest part of the church – and rounded arches, pointing the way to the Renaissance, in the nave and transept. The star vault is magnificent. The real highlight of the interior is the ★★ **Renaissance rood screen** (1541). The stained-glass windows in the ambulatory are also very fine; they evince both Late Gothic and Renaissance design influences.

The ★ **Jardin du Luxembourg** is an oasis of peace and tranquillity. It was laid out in its present-day form by Chalgrin at the end of the 18th century, when it was extended considerably. The sculptures were added later, in the 19th century. The southernmost end of the park is rounded off by Carpeaux's ★ **Fontaine de l'Observatoire**, with its allegorical female figures representing the four continents. A few steps further on, past the Place Julian, is the Monument du Maréchal Ney by François Rude (1853). Ney was one of Napoleon's most famous generals. Condemned to death for high treason after the Battle of Waterloo, he was shot on this spot on 7 December 1815.

To the north of the park is the **Palais du Luxembourg** ❻❼. This building, constructed for Marie de Médicis after the murder of her husband Henry IV, was modelled after the Palazzo Pitti in Florence. Salomon de Brosse received the commission. It remained a royal palace until the revolution. Since 1800 the *palais* has housed the French Senate, the highest legislative body in the land.

The widowed queen moved into the palais when it was still unfinished, in 1625. She left the neighbouring *Petit-Palais* to Richelieu, who was soon to become her bitter enemy. In 1631, with the support of her son Louis XIII, he forced her into exile. She died in Cologne in 1642, lonely and understandably embittered.

Permission for individual or group guided tours must be obtained from the Sécrétariat General de la Questure du Senat, 15 Rue de Vaugirard, F-75006 Paris. The main highlights of the conducted tour are the Salle d'Or, which still retains its original painted ceilings and panelling, the 19th-century neoclassical staircase by Chalgrin in the right wing, and the fresco by Eugène Delacroix in the library's reading-room.

The adjacent Petit Luxembourg is the official home of the president of the Senate. It is open to visitors.

North of the Jardin du Luxembourg, on the Place St-Sulpice, is the Church of **St-Sulpice** 68. A parish church for the local peasantry stood on this spot as long ago as the 12th century. In 1646, Anne of Austria laid the foundation-stone for a new building of larger dimensions. Construction work continued until 1736, with several interruptions. The commission for the facade, which was still missing, went to the Italian architect Giovanni Niccoló Servandoni. On his death in 1766 the severe and monumental two-storey facade, which dominates the square, was complete except for the upper towers. The left-hand tower was completed in 1777 by Chalgrin, the architect who built the Arc de Triomphe.

The dimensions of the interior, too, are quite overwhelming (118m/385ft) long, 57m/187ft) wide and 34m/110ft high). Despite the various interruptions during its construction, the church conveys an architectural unity. The most dominant features are the high pilasters between the archways, with the massive barrel vault high above. Highlights here include the brilliantly executed altar statue of the Virgin in St Mary's Chapel and also the ★ **frescoes** by Delacroix in the first of the southern chapels, which include *Jacob Wrestling with the Angel*. The organ-loft with its pillars was designed by Chalgrin (1776) and public recitals are often given.

St-Germain-des-Prés, interior

The church of ★★ **St-Germain-des-Prés** 69, which has the oldest bell-tower in all of Paris, lies on the tiny Place St-Germain-des-Prés, very close to such renowned institutions as **Café de Flore** and **Aux Deux Magots**, where the existentialists once used to meet.

The church's predecessor was a Merovingian mausoleum. A Benedictine abbey then developed here with its own jurisdiction, independent of the secular authorities, and only answerable to the Pope. Surrounded by a ring of fortifications, it lay in the middle of the suburb of Bourg St-Germain until the 17th century. The walls were only finally demolished when the elegant Faubourg St-Germain was constructed. St-Germain-des-Prés celebrated its heyday during the High Middle Ages and during the 17th century, when the abbey produced a number of scholars of European importance.

Romanesque nave,
St-Germain-des-Prés

The oldest section of the building is the massive west wing which dates from around AD1000. The tower's upper floor is 12th-century, though the helm roof had to be renewed in the 19th century, when a great deal of restoration to the fabric of the church took place. The nave and transept are the only Romanesque church interiors left in Paris. Both originally had flat ceilings; the vault was only added in the 17th century. The tombstones of the Merovingian kings buried here were transferred to St-Denis (where the French kings and high-ranking members of the nobility have been buried since Dagobert's time).

One very rewarding way to round off this tour is to take a detour to the attractive Place Furstenberg. House No 6 was formerly the studio of artist Eugène Delacroix, and has been converted into a museum (daily except Tuesday and public holidays 9.45am–12.30pm and 2–5.15pm, weekends from 9.45am–5.15pm).

Opposite the Louvre, and still on the left bank of the Seine, is the **Institut de France ⑳**. Designed by palace architect Louis Le Vau to harmonise with the architecture of The Louvre, it was built between 1662 and 1691. It consists of five academies, the most famous of which is the **Académie Française**, founded in 1635 by Cardinal Richelieu with the aim of maintaining the integrity of the French language and compiling an official dictionary. Its 40 members (they are limited to that number), nicknamed 'the immortals', hold their meetings beneath the large dome. The assembly hall contains the memorial to Cardinal Mazarin by Antoine Coysevox (1692).

The interior may only be visited with prior permission from the relevant authorities (23 Quai Conti).

Dancing on the Pont des Arts

Route 9

★★★ Eiffel Tower – ★★★ Musée d'Orsay (*Métro Trocadéro, lines 6 and 9; bus Nos 22, 30, 32, 63, 82*)

The view of the Eiffel Tower from the Palais de Chaillot

The starting-point for this route is the ★ **Place du Trocadéro** with the equestrian statue of Maréchal Foch. From the terrace of the ★ **Palais de Chaillot ⓲** there is a magnificent view of the Champ-de-Mars lower down, and of the Eiffel Tower. A small country house belonging to Cathérine de Médicis used to stand on this spot. Later it belonged to the Marshal des Bassompière, who was imprisoned in the Bastille by Richelieu because of his dissolute lifestyle. Henrietta, the widow of Charles I of England and sister of Louis XIII, had the house turned into a convent. According to contemporary chronicles, it provided numerous princesses and ladies of the nobility with a welcome, albeit temporary, respite from Richelieu's strong moral codes of conduct.

Napoleon wanted a castle built on the site for his son, the king of Rome, but by the time he fell from power only the initial foundations had been laid. The only section to be completed was the bridge leading up to it, the Pont d'Iéna. In 1827 the hill here was named the Trocadéro, in memory of the Spanish fortress of the same name which had been taken by the French in 1823. For the international exhibition of 1878 the Palais du Trocadéro was constructed, an imaginative and somewhat bizarre-looking circular building with a Moorish dome, which had to make way for the new Palais de Chaillot in 1937.

Sculptural detail, Palais de Chaillot

Built in the shape of an amphitheatre, the wings of the Palais follow the original outline of the old Trocadéro ground-plan. The main part of the building lies below the huge viewing terrace.

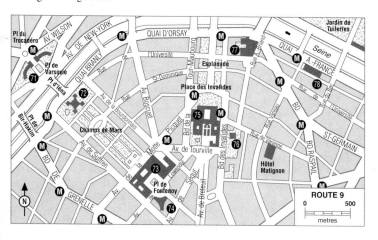

ROUTE 9

0 — 500

metres

Palais de Chaillot from the Eiffel Tower

From the Musée de Monuments

The Eiffel Tower

The Palais de Chaillot today contains four separate and very different museums (daily except Tuesday and public holidays, times vary, but 10am–4pm as a rule; except Musée de Cinéma: guided tours only, 10am, 11am, 2pm, 3pm and 4pm):

★ **Musée des Monuments Français**: reproductions of French monuments, from the Merovingian period to the 19th century.

Musée de la Marine: history of the French navy and also the French merchant navy, with numerous models of ships.

Musée de l'Homme: prehistoric, anthropological and palaeontological collections.

Musée du Cinéma Henri Langlois: an exhibition documenting the history of motion pictures.

The whole area is completely dominated by the ★★★ **Eiffel Tower ❼❷**. This 300-m (984-ft) high tower is one of the most famous tourist attractions in the world. It was built according to plans by architect Gustave Eiffel between 28 January 1887 and 31 March 1889 for the Paris International Exhibition of 1889. The first transoceanic radio contact was made from here in 1916, and radio programmes have been broadcast from the Eiffel Tower ever since then. The 20.75-m (68-ft) high television antenna was erected in 1957. The uppermost platform contains a meteorological station as well as electronic equipment used for air traffic control.

The tower weighs only 7,000 tons, and consists of around 12,000 individual steel sections. Fifty-two tons of paint are needed to give it just one coat. Despite its massive dimensions, the weight of the Eiffel Tower is distributed in such a way that each square centimetre of ground area is only subjected to 4kg (8.8lbs) of pressure (roughly equivalent to the weight of an average person sitting on a chair). Even during the fiercest storms, the top of the tower never moves more than 12cm (4.7ins).

The first platform, where there is a restaurant, is 57m (187ft) up. The second platform, also with a restaurant, is 115m (377ft) above the ground. There are 1,652 steps leading from the bottom to the very top of the tower. From the second platform, a lift takes visitors up to the third one, 300m (984ft) above the ground.

Between the Eiffel Tower and the Military Academy is the 1-km (0.6-mile) long and 250-m (820-ft) wide ★ **Champ de Mars**, formerly used for troop manoeuvres and military exercises under the *ancien régime*. Today it forms the green heart of a highly desirable residential area. The Champ de Mars was the scene of early experiments in aviation as long ago as the 18th century: the French physicist Jacques Alexandre César Charles made the first ever ascent in a hydrogen balloon here in 1783. One year later Blanchard attempted a similar ascent with a balloon he claimed could be steered.

In the Champ des Mars

Beyond, on the Avenue de la Motte Piquet, lies the **Ecole Militaire** ❼❸. Madame de Pompadour, the mistress of Louis XV, had the idea of constructing an architectural monument in honour of the king. It was to be modelled after the Hôtel des Invalides, and the architect Jacques-Ange Gabriel was entrusted with the project. Money was scarce, and the building took a long time to complete. In 1773 the main part of the structure was ready, and the courtyard of honour one year later. Further additions were made in 1782, 1856 and 1865. But the costly military school was short-lived – it only lasted until 1787, and its most famous pupil was Napoleon Bonaparte. Today, alongside the military academy, the building houses several other academic institutions.

The Ecole Militaire

The south front of the building, with its colossal portico and massive dome, faces the Champ de Mars. The main facade, with its Cour d'Honneur enclosed by colonnades, borders the Avenue de Lowendal. The interior, which unfortunately can only be visited by permission of the military authorities (1 Place Joffre) and then only as part of a conducted tour, contains almost entirely original decoration.

On the south side of the Place de Fontenoy stands the **Maison de L'UNESCO** ❼❹. A combined achievement of the member states, this building, which was erected in 1958, was designed by Marcel Breuer (US), Bernhard Zehrfuss (France) and Pier Luigi Nervi (Italy). The ground-plan of the seven-storey building is Y-shaped. Artists of several different nationalities were commissioned to do the interior decoration for the conference building, designed by Nervi. The wall painting is by Picasso (*Victory of Light and Peace over Darkness and*

Hôtel des Invalides

Death). The mural in the conference room is by Mexican artist Rufino Tamayo *(Prometheus Bringing Fire to Man)*. The library contains several bronze reliefs by Jean Arp. There are Joan Miró ceramics and in the garden there is a Henry Moore sculpture *(Reclining Figure Resting)*.

At the end of the Avenue de Breteuil is the eye-catching and enormous silhouette of the Dôme des Invalides at the rear of the ★★ **Hôtel des Invalides** ㉝, the main facade of which faces the Seine. In 1670, at the suggestion of his minister Louvois, Louis XIV took the step, unparalleled in Europe at that time, of founding a charitable institution for disabled ex-servicemen, who until then had had to rely on the benevolence of monasteries.

The Hôtel des Invalides was built between 1671 and 1675 as a home for war veterans, and soon provided shelter for 6,000 ex-servicemen and hospital staff.

Gilded cherubs, Dôme des Invalides

64

★★ **Dôme des Invalides** (daily 10am–5pm). The Eglise du Dôme contrasts in shape and colour with the rest of the complex. Unlike the soldiers' church behind it, the Dôme (1680–1706) was planned not for religious services, but simply as a tomb for the Sun King.

Designed by the architect Hardouin-Mansart, the church is considered to be a masterpiece of the French baroque-classical style. The interior was modelled after Michelangelo's design for St Peter's in Rome, and an opening in the inner dome reveals a richly painted outer dome, lit by hidden windows – a typical baroque effect. Stairways on either side of the baldachin altar lead down to the crypt. The antechamber contains the tombs of major-domos Bertrand – who followed the emperor into exile – and Duroc.

On the inner walls of the crypt, neoclassical reliefs portray the glorious deeds of Napoleon and in front of a niche-statue of the emperor lies the tomb of his son, the King of Rome and later Duke of Reichsstadt. Twelve winged victories representing Napoleon's glorious campaigns surround the ambulatory; in the centre is the enormous porphyry sarcophagus containing Napoleon's mortal remains – which are actually inside the innermost of a total of six coffins made of different materials.

The chapels also include the sarcophagi of Joseph Bonaparte (King of Naples), Jérôme Bonaparte (King of Westphalia) and Maréchal Foch (commander-in-chief of the French troops in World War I).

The Cour d'Honneur

The main portal to the Place des Invalides leads to the **Cour d'Honneur** (Courtyard of Honour). There used to be dining-halls and kitchens on the ground floor, and bedrooms higher up. Beyond, along the 16-m (50-ft) long corridors, were the hospital wards with apothecaries, laboratories, etc. Today the building is used by the army administration, and also houses the **Musée de l'Armée** (daily 10am–5pm).

The interior of **St-Louis-des-Invalides** (known as the soldiers' church) is unassuming and devoid of decoration except for military banners. The central aisle supports a barrel vault. It was here that the first performance of Berlioz's *Requiem* took place, in 1837.

The Hôtel Biron at No 7 Rue de Varenne houses the ★★ **Musée Rodin** **76** (daily except Monday 10am–5.15pm, in summer until 6pm; closed 1 January and 1 May). The famous sculptor lived on the ground floor of this building from 1910 until his death in 1917. His apartment was then turned into a museum, and contains his life's work (including *The Thinker* and *The Burghers of Calais*) as well as his own private art collection.

Exhibits, Musée Rodin

The large complex of buildings making up the ★ **Palais Bourbon** **77** lies at the junction of the Rue A. Briand/Rue de l'Université/Quai d'Orsay. Also known as the Chamber of Deputies, this building has been the seat of the Assemblée Nationale (National Assembly) since 1871.

At the core of this complex is the Hôtel Bourbon. It was begun as a one-storey garden palace for the Duchesse de Bourbon in 1732, and the gardens extended as far as the Seine. In 1765 extra storeys were built, and Napoleon I had the temple facade added between 1804 and 1807.

The former railway station of ★ **Gare d'Orsay** **78**, with its ironwork, is a typical example of the architectural style of the Belle Epoque. It was opened punctually on the 14 July national holiday in 1900, for the international exhibition of that year. The Gare d'Orsay escaped demolition in 1973 thanks to a theatre group who took it over, and then in 1977 the decision was made to turn it into an art museum for the period 1848–1914. The masterpieces of France's leading Impressionist painters have been on display at the ★★★ **Musée d'Orsay** in the Rue de Bellechasse (Tuesday, Wednesday, Friday, Saturday 10am–6pm, Sunday 9am–6pm, Thursday 10am–9.45pm; 20 June to 20 September from 9am; closed Monday) since its official opening at the end of 1986.

Musée d'Orsay

Monet, Manet, Renoir, Pissarro, Sisley, Degas, etc are all represented here (upper floor), as are Neo-Impressionists Seurat and Signac, and also artists who paved the way for modern painting, such as Gauguin and Van Gogh. The 32-m (100-ft) high and 138-m (450-ft) long former ticket hall of the station has been impressively transformed into a kind of 'sculpture avenue' (Rodin, Carpeaux, Rude, etc). There are a total of 17,000sq metres (20,300sq yds) of exhibition space available here for sculpture, painting, architecture, poster art, early film, urban architecture and city planning. The museum also has an extensive library with a documentation centre, and an auditorium as well as a rooftop café with a splendid view across Paris.

65

La Ruche

Route 10

★★ **Montparnasse** *(Métro Montparnasse-Bienvenue, Vavin, lines 4, 6, 12 and 13; bus Nos 28, 48, 82, 89, 91, 92, 94, 95, 96)*

Café, Montparnasse

This area has been inhabited by students since the 17th century. Inspired by Greek mythology and by the hill which used to be here, they named this part of the city Parnasse (Parnassus) after the seat of Apollo. The hill was later removed. Montparnasse celebrated its real heyday towards the end of the 19th century.

The first famous resident was the painter Henri Rousseau, and he was followed by many sculptors, writers, poets and artists. The establishment known as **La Ruche** (The Beehive) at No 52 Rue de Dantzig soon became as famous as the Bateau-Lavoir at Montmartre before it. Cafés such as Le Dôme, La Coupole, La Rotonde and Dupont were frequented by Russian émigrés like Lenin and Trotsky, and composers such as Stravinsky. Numerous artists still live and work at La Ruche even today. Between the two world wars in particular, Montparnasse was the meeting-place for writers who would later achieve worldwide fame, such as Ernest Hemingway, Henry Miller, André Gide, Paul Verlaine and Louis Aragon. The Closerie des Lilas (No 171 Boulevard de Montparnasse) was one of their favourite haunts.

After World War II the city planners began an ambitious redevelopment project, the most visible symbol of which is the Maine-Montparnasse skyscraper.

The starting-point for this route is the station of Montparnasse. Right outside it is the enormous ★ **Tour Maine-Montparnasse** ⑲ (summer, daily 9.30am–11.30pm;

winter, weekdays only until 10.30pm). This skyscraper, 210m (690ft) high, was the highest in Europe when it was completed in 1973. Fifty-two of the 58 floors contain offices. The entire edifice uses up as much power as a town with 30,000 inhabitants. The foundations had to be rammed 70m (220ft) into the earth in order to support the building's 120,000-ton weight.

View from Tour Montparnasse

From the terrace up on the roof and also from the restaurant on the 56th storey there is a superb view of Paris and, in good weather, of much of the Ile de France. The lift takes just one minute to reach the top.

At the back of the skyscraper is a shopping centre and the Place du 18 Juin 1940. The name commemorates the day on which General de Gaulle, in a radio message from London, urged the French to resist the Germans : 'We have lost a battle, but not the war.'

No 16 Rue Antoine-Bourdelle, the former home of Rodin's pupil Antoine Bourdelle (1861–1929), houses the ★★ **Musée Bourdelle** ⓮ (daily except Monday and public holidays 10am–5.40pm). The artist's former studio and his garden contain a magnificent collection of hundreds of his sculptures, paintings and drawings.

Sculpture, Musée Bourdelle

67

Stamp collectors should definitely visit the **Musée de la Poste** ⓮ (daily except Sunday and public holidays 10am–6pm) at No 34 Boulevard Vaugirard. This museum contains a well documented exhibition showing the development of the postal service from the 15th century to the present day, including special wartime services. The gallery has a display of postage stamp art.

The Rue du Docteur Roux contains one of the finest medical institutes in the world, the **Institut Pasteur** ⓮ (daily except Saturday, Sunday and public holidays

Louis Pasteur

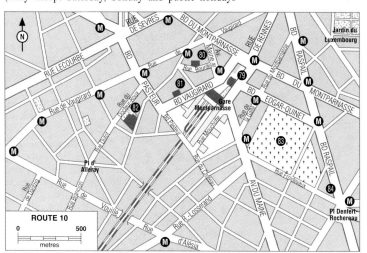

Cimetière de Montparnasse

2–5.30pm. Films and lectures are also available on request). Research laboratories and a clinic for infectious diseases are all housed in this complex, as well as a library and lecture theatres. There is also a museum, recreating the home of famous bacteriologist Louis Pasteur (1822–95). His tomb is in the basement, in a special Byzantine-style crypt.

The Avenue du Maine leads on to the **Rue de la Gaîté**, which used to be famous during the heyday of Montparnasse. Establishments such as La Mère Cadet, Le Veau qui Tête and Le Bal des Gigoteurs were just as well-known as the restaurants Milles Colonnes (No 20), Gaîté Montparnasse (No 26), the Music Hall Bobino (No 20) and the Théâtre Montparnasse (No 31).

Skulls in the catacombs

The Rue de la Gaîté continues on as far as the Boulevard Edgar Quinet, and the **Cimetière de Montparnasse** ㉝, the third largest graveyard in Paris (18ha/14.4 acres), laid out in 1824. Among those buried here are the sculptors François Rude (1784–1855) and Antoine Bourdelle (1861–1929) (his grave bears no inscription and lies next to the wall opposite area 9); and writers Guy de Maupassant (1850–93), Charles Baudelaire (1821–67), Jean-Paul Sartre (1905–80) and Simone de Beauvoir (1908–86).

After a walk through this graveyard, a visit to the **Catacombs** ㉞ (Tuesday to Friday 2pm–4pm, Saturday and Sunday 9am–11am and 2pm–4pm) should not be missed. They are at the Place Denfert-Rochereau, beneath the Métro station of the same name. There were subterranean quarries here in Gallo-Roman times. After the cemeteries in the city centre were closed in 780, around 6 million skeletons were brought here. The bones are piled up in the galleries along the winding passageways. Danton and Robespierre were supposedly buried here, and it was the Resistance headquarters during World War II.

Additional Sights

The following sights and excursion destinations, alphabetically arranged, can be reached from the city centre either by private car or by public transport.

Arènes de Lutèce

47 Rue Monge and Rue de Navarre, Métro Monge, Jussieu; bus Nos 47, 67 89

Arènes de Lutece

The amphitheatre of the Roman settlement of Lutetia was built in around AD200, but after the barbarian invasion in 285 it was used as a quarry. When the Rue Monge was built during the reign of Napoleon III, the ruins were found.

The amphitheatre covers a surface area of 100m (320ft) x 130m (425ft), which is almost equal to that of the theatre in Nîmes. Seventeen hundred spectators – roughly the entire population of the Roman settlement of that time – could sit here and watch gladiators, as well as theatre or circus performances.

Today the two large entrances to the arena are still clearly recognisable, as are the rows of seats – including individual ones with their occupants' names scratched into them. The stage and the actors' dressing-rooms at the back are also visible. The broken sections of squared-stone masonry were once used to keep the poles supporting the sun-roof in position.

69

★★ Bois de Boulogne

Métro Porte Maillot, line 1, Porte Dauphine, line 2, Porte d'Auteuil, line 10

In the Bois de Boulogne

This huge area of forest contains not only the palace of Bagatelle that once belonged to the Duke of Artois (entrance on the Route de Longchamps) but also the two famous racetracks Auteuil and Longchamps, as well as the Palais de Congrès. The Bois de Boulogne is a favourite excursion destination for the Parisians. A tour on foot around it, including the two lakes (Lac Inférieur and Lac Supérieur), takes about three hours.

★ La Défense

Métro Grande Arche de la Défense, line 1; RER La Défense, line A, bus No 73

La Défense lies to the west of the city, beyond the Pont de Neuilly and the Seine. The complex that makes up this satellite city symbolises France's architectural breakthrough into the 21st century. *Défense* is the name of the bronze sculpture by Barrias that was erected on the square in 1883, and which is now surrounded by around 750ha (1,859 acres) of modern architecture. The sculpture commemorates the defence of Paris against the Prussian army during the war of 1870.

Grande Arche, La Défense

Around 100,000 people work here, and nearly 30,000 live here. The area contains all the necessary modern conveniences and entertainment facilities, schools, sports grounds and also a park.

One of the most distinctive buildings, the ★ **Centre International des Industries et Techniques** (CNIT) was converted into a hotel with a congress centre. The 90,000-sq m (107,600-sq yd) roof (larger than the Place de la Concorde) is supported by only three arches spanning 284m (930ft). To the west, rounding off the view along the Louvre–Arc de Triomphe–La Défense axis is the ★★ **Grande Arche**, a monumental marble gate 110m (360ft) high and 106m (345ft) wide. The Human Rights Foundation is one of the institutions housed beneath its roof. The dark glass towers of insurance companies jostle for attention with the colossal oil company buildings and hotels, flashing in the sunlight. The huge Quatre Temps department store lies at the heart of this designer city, which stares down proudly – but also somewhat enviously – at the lively old metropolis spread out beneath its feet.

Egouts (the Paris sewers)

Métro Alma-Marceau; RER Pont de l'Alma
The entrance is on the Place de la Résistance near the Pont de l'Alma. Beneath the entire city is a massive system of subterranean passageways, quarries, sewers, installations for fresh water, piping, etc. Conducted tours daily except Thursday and Friday, 11am–5pm.

Euro Disney

RER Marne de Vallée–Chessy– Euro Disney; A4 motorway (Metz-Nancy)
This colossal entertainment park covers 20sq km (7.7sq miles) – equivalent to one-fifth of the Paris metropolitan area – and lies 32km (20 miles) to the east of the capital near the town of Marne-la-Vallée.

The Mosque

★ Mosquée (Mosque)

10 Rue Georges-Desplas, Métro Jussieu; bus Nos 67, 91
This mosque was built in the Moorish-Spanish style in 1922–6 for Muslims living in France. The minaret towering above the complex is 33m (110ft) high. In the middle of the courtyard, which is surrounded by double pillars, stands the fountain for ritual ablutions. The Hall of Prayer to the west, laid with magnificent carpets, contains the distinctive *mihrab* (prayer niche) facing southeast (towards Mecca) and the *mimbar*, a pulpit for Friday sermons. Two enormous wall panels bear the names of Allah and the Holy Prophet Mohammed in Arabic writing. Shoes need to be removed and placed by the entrance before the Hall of Prayer may be entered.

On the other side of the courtyard is the Islamic Institute for Religious Science. Inside the buildings to the south of it are a *hammam* (hot baths), a *souk* (bazaar), a Moorish café and a restaurant.

Observatory (Observatoire)
61 Avenue de l'Observatoire, RER Port-Royal; bus Nos 38, 83, 91

Constructed by Claude Perrault (1667–72), this building is intersected in the middle by the Paris Meridian (2°20'1" east of Greenwich). The four facades face the four points of the compass. Its south side lies on the latitude of Paris (48°50'11" north). By prior arrangement, there is a tour every Saturday at 2pm through the small astronomical museum.

★ Père-Lachaise
Boulevard de Ménilmontant, Métro Père-Lachaise

The largest graveyard in Paris. Among those buried here are Chopin, Beaumarchais, Balzac, Bizet, Sarah Bernhardt, Bellini, Cherubini, Oscar Wilde, Molière, La Fontaine, Colette, Edith Piaf and Jim Morrison, whose grave has become a shrine for his fans.

Jim Morrison's grave, Père Lachaise

71

★ La Villette
Métro Porte de la Villette/Porte de Pantin

Between the Canal St-Denis and the Canal de l'Ourcq, on the site of the former abattoirs and cattle-markets of La Villette, an ambitious exhibition and leisure park has been laid out covering 55ha (136 acres) (daily except Monday, 10am–6pm). It includes the Cité des Sciences et de l'Industrie, a state-of-the-art museum of science and industry built with the aim of introducing visitors to the world of technology. There is a permanent exhibition here with experimental installations, a planetarium, a media library and an area especially designed for children.

Behind the main hall stands *La Géode* (daily except Monday). This enormous hollow steel ball composed of 6,433 stainless-steel triangles beneath an outer covering and measuring 36m (118ft) in diameter is an architectural masterpiece: it contains one of the largest film screens in the world (1,000sq m/1,196sq yds), forming a hemisphere 26m (85ft) in diameter. Scientific films are shown here, always starting on the hour.

La Géode at La Villette

The Grande Halle, a fine example of 19th-century iron architecture, is no longer used as a cattle hall. Today, exhibitions and cultural events are held here.

The La Villette complex also includes a park covering 35ha (86 acres), the Zénith concert hall and a theatre as well as the Cité de la Musique to the south, the seat of the Paris Conservatoire.

Art and Culture

Roman Lutetia

Paris, with its two million inhabitants, originated on the Ile de la Cité, the island in the Seine settled in the 3rd century BC by the Celtic tribe of the Parisii, who built a fortified settlement, Lucotesia (Midwater Dwelling).

In 52 BC, while Julius Caesar was conquering Gaul, the Celtic settlement was destroyed (*see Historical Summary*), and a Roman colonial town was built on its ruins. Its centre lay not on the island, but on the slopes of Mont Ste-Geneviève. The ruins of the thermal baths have been preserved at the Hôtel de Cluny on the Rue des Arènes. The main axis of the rectangular Roman street grid was the road already in existence that led from Orléans in the south to Senlis in the north, crossing the Seine via wooden bridges near the Ile de la Cité. *Lutetia Parisiorum* was a Roman provincial town for 300 years, until attacks by Germanic tribes towards the end of the 3rd century AD made it necessary to fortify the Ile de la Cité and shift the population behind the protecting walls. It was in this *palatium* – later the island's palace – in February 360 that Julian the Apostate was appointed emperor of Rome. He tried to abolish Christianity (officially tolerated since 313) and restore the ancient gods.

The first Christian communities in Paris probably existed from as early as the mid-3rd century. Around the year 250 St Dionysius came to Paris as a Gallic missionary, and there may already have been a cathedral on the island in the Seine at that time. After his martyrdom he was buried on the site of the abbey that was later to become the last resting-place of the French kings – St Denis, north of Paris

The Merovingians

During the 4th and 5th century the Franks gradually conquered more and more territory. In 486 the Merovingian Clovis removed the last bastion of Roman rule and turned the centre of Gaul into a Frankish kingdom. In 498 he converted to the Christian faith, ushering in the Christianisation of the Franks. In 508 he shifted his residence to Paris, which became the secular and spiritual centre of the Frankish Empire.

The Roman palatium became a Merovingian imperial palace, and a series of monastic communities sprang up across the fields and meadows, including what would later become St-Germain-des-Prés (several Merovingian kings are buried within its walls). The foundation of St-Pierre-et-St-Paul also dates back to Clovis' time; it was consecrated to Paris's most popular saint, the nun Geneviève (Ste-Geneviève), who according to legend protected Paris from invasion by Attila the Hun in 451.

*Opposite:
Notre-Dame de Paris*

Celtic coinage

Gallo-Roman ruins

5th-century pendant

The emergence of France

The Carolingians, who dethroned the Merovingians for good in 751, no longer resided in Paris. Counts were appointed to govern the city as *prévôts* (provosts). By the year 800, Paris was already an important trading centre with a population of around 25,000. In the 9th century the city suffered yet again, this time from attacks by the Normans. It was only in 885–6 that Parisian Count Eudes succeeded in repelling another attack by building fortifications around the Cité. He was promptly crowned king of France in 888 at Compiègne after Charles III, king of the Western Franks, had been removed from power. The power struggle between the Carolingians and Eudes' successors, the Robertians, ended with a victory for the Parisian counts. Count Hugo Capet, pronounced king in 987, was the first of a long line of Capetian kings that was to last until the revolution. From now on the history of Paris was inseparable from the history of the French crown – similar to the role played by Rome in the ancient Roman Empire.

In the 11th century the city grew very rapidly indeed. The monumental churches built in Paris in the mid-12th century could not, of course, rival the magnificent Romanesque churches of Burgundy or Normandy. St-Germain-des-Prés and the choir of St-Martin-des-Champs are the only structures to have survived from that time.

Gothic vaulting, St-Denis

The Gothic period

This all changed abruptly with the development of an architectural style in the Ile de France – the crown lands around Paris – that was closely associated with the claim to power of the Capetian kings. The first programmatic plan for a Gothic structure was designed by Abbot Suger for the choir of St-Denis (construction work began in 1140), which as the burial-place of kings and repository of the royal regalia had become a French national monument. Abbot Suger, the king's friend and adviser, consciously aimed at a new architectural style that would serve as a model for the royal demesne. Structural innovations that had developed elsewhere, such as the pointed arch and the ribbed vault, were now combined to create an entirely new style.

The Gothic cathedral, which originated in this way, is distinctive for its twin-towered, three-storeyed west facade with its rose window at the centre, and also its three portals, surrounded by statues and reliefs dealing with the theme of salvation and redemption, in an attempt to put the visitor in the right frame of mind before entering. The interior contains a long nave, opening out towards the side aisles by means of arcades with pointed arches. Above the pillars in the nave arcade, rounded and tapering piers blend

harmoniously into the ribbed vault above. Broad, high, stained-glass windows fill the spaces in between. The mystically flowing, colourful and sparkling light was supposed to symbolise the light of heaven, just as the numeric symbolism of the geometrical relationships was meant to evoke the harmony of the House of God on Earth. At their narrow ends, the transepts have their own separate entrances, and then there is the dazzling choir, its ambulatory and ring of chapels making it resemble a monstrance. Instead of being supported by massive walls, the weight of the roof is born by flying buttresses outside the building, their magnificence harmonising with the artistic effect of the structure as a whole.

The choir and stained-glass in St-Denis

75

Only a few sections of Suger's original building survive today. The Early Gothic cathedral of Notre-Dame (1163) is a far better place to gain an impression of the new style. There is much here that is hesitant and undeveloped compared with the High Gothic style of Rheims Cathedral: the nave is broken up rather too often, and there is not enough light in the building – despite later alterations. The west facade, however, radiates perfection and harmony, even though it took so long to build: around the huge rose window, surfaces blend into each other with beautiful simplicity and clarity.

Ever since the end of the 12th century the city had been forming into three distinct parts: *la ville* on the right bank, the centre of trade, with the market at its centre that would later become Les Halles; *la cité*, with the cathedral and the royal residence; and the *université* on the left bank, the centre of scholasticism.

It was in the mid-13th century that the most magnificent examples of High Gothic appeared in Paris: the filigree transept of Notre-Dame with its fine tracery, and the superb interior of the Sainte-Chapelle, the court chapel built

Notre-Dame, transept

Sainte-Chappelle, interior

16th-century facade of the Palais du Louvre

St-Eustache

on the site of the former royal palace on the Cité by Saint Louis, to house his reliquaries. Here the dividing wall seems to have vanished completely. The ribbed vault soars above on narrow piers rising up from the floor, and the 15-m (49-ft) high stained-glass window dominates the interior of the building.

The handful of Late Gothic parish churches that survive from this uneasy period – the monasteries built by the various orders were torn down during the revolution – reveal a heavy dependence on High Gothic forms, with much that is dry and lacklustre. The only real innovation is the Flamboyant style of tracery, distinguished by a passion for the ogee, or 's'-shaped curve. Two very fine Late Gothic palaces, the Hôtel de Sens and the Hôtel de Cluny, date from the end of the 15th century when Paris was slowly recovering from war, plague and famine – both have been extensively restored.

The Renaissance

The return of Francis I (1515–47) to Paris from Italy marked the beginning of a new epoch. The king introduced the Renaissance forms developed in Italy, and the adaptation of the national Gothic tradition to antique pillars and cornices resulted in a typically French facade style. From the very start the full-bodied Italian forms were used to create artistic and elegant surface decoration. Walls remained emphatically flat, windows high and narrow. The steep Gothic roof, in particular, was retained in preference to the Italian flat one. In 1528 Italian artists were involved when construction work began on the palace at Fontainebleau, and from 1547 onwards the new Palais du Louvre, designed by Lescot and with fine facade reliefs by Jean Goujon, was built on the site of the former fortress. Two churches, though still very Gothic, reveal the originality of the adaptation of Italian forms: St-Eustache (1532) and St-Etienne-du-Mont.

These new forces were hindered from full development in the 16th century, however, by the Wars of Religion between the Catholic League and the Protestant Huguenots, culminating in 1572 in the Massacre of St Bartholomew's Day, when around 3,000 Huguenots perished. Peace only returned to Paris with the accession to the throne of Henry IV (1589–1610), who successfully rebuilt and extended the city: during the 16th century its population doubled to more than 400,000.

Henry IV's reign also heralded the epoch of systematic town planning – an attempt to get Paris' rapid expansion under control. Straight streets lined with uniform facades were introduced as a counterpart to the maze of medieval alleyways. A uniform system of squares was also introduced: these included the Place Dauphine with the

Pont Neuf (the first modern bridge, without any houses on it, and now the oldest surviving bridge in Paris), and also the Place Royale (today's Place des Vosges), which were both surrounded by a series of uniform facades.

The Place des Vosges went on to become the centre of the Marais quarter and of aristocratic life; several *hôtels particuliers* (palaces owned by the nobility) were built in its immediate vicinity. These buildings are all of the same type: a main building *(corps de logis)* with low wings surrounding a courtyard *(cour d'honneur)* divided off from the street by a wall, and with a garden at the back. From 1612 these unpretentious palace facades of the type surrounding the Place des Vosges gave rise to the style of house widespread in France with its walls of red brick and its white stone quoins (solid-corner angles) and window surrounds, beneath a steep slate-grey roof.

Place des Vosges

The grand siècle

Under Louis XIII (1610–43) and his minister Richelieu, the king's divine right and absolute authority was proclaimed, and the nobility was gradually deprived of its political rights – a policy which was continued by Cardinal Mazarin (1643–61), chief adviser to the young Louis XIV. An eventual rebellion by the nobility (the Frondes) against the absolutist monarchy, was finally crushed once and for all in 1653.

The citizens' fanatical Catholicism meant that Paris developed into a centre of the Counter-Reformation in the first half of the 17th century. Sixty new monasteries and 20 churches were built with the aim of turning Paris into a second Rome, and they included some of France's most important religious structures: the Jesuit Church of St-Paul-St-Louis, the Church of the Sorbonne by Lemercier and the masterly Val-de-Grâce by Lemercier and François Mansart. They were all modelled on the Roman baroque church, with its two-storey gabled and pillared facade, its broad, barrel-vaulted nave flanked by chapels, and its high cupola above the crossing, flooded with light. What makes these buildings so typically French is their atmosphere of restrained vigour and the exemplary harmony and balance of their external appearance; this reached the peak of perfection in the Dôme des Invalides, begun under Louis XIV in 1680.

The facade of Val-de-Grâce

French art entered its classical phase, the *grand style*, during the reign of Louis XIV (1643–1715), the Sun King, a period that also marked the high point of centralised state power and of French pre-eminence in Europe. At the centre of royal artistic policy stood the Palace of Versailles (1671), symbolising the absolute power of the monarch. It began on the site of a modest royal hunting lodge and grew to become the biggest palace in Europe. Louis Le

Vau, Hardouin-Mansart and Charles Lebrun designed the great palace and André Le Nôtre laid out the magnificent formal gardens. Construction work on the palace and its grounds continued after the king's death in 1715, and used up incredible sums of money. Members of the academy appointed by the king determined the principles of *le bon goût* (good taste) in architecture and art – and the principles were binding. The result was a unified architecture and art right across France. Nevertheless, there was nothing academic about the Louis XIV style: the king's classical, anti-baroque attitude – clearly expressed in Perrault's dignified Louvre colonnade – combined solemnity with ceremonial severity, restrained vigour and intellectual clarity.

Louix XIV as a Roman emperor

Under the influence of the king's finance minister, Colbert, Paris experienced an architectural *embellissement* (embellishment), and programmes were also introduced to further improve hygiene, security, employment and social welfare. The king's closest artistic advisers, Le Nôtre, Le Vau, Hardouin-Mansart and the painter Lebrun, were appointed to oversee the changes. In a self-confident gesture of royal unassailability, the city walls were removed, and broad avenues *(boulevards)* took their place. The city gates were replaced by triumphal arches. The Place des Victoires and the Place Vendôme were redesigned as royal squares and were provided with statues as centrepieces, the Louvre was extended, and the addition of the Tuileries and the Champs-Elysées as far as the Rond-Point created a 'Royal Axis'.

Rue de la Paix in the 18th century

The 18th century

During the regency and reign of Louis XV (1715–74) state finances were so depleted that no major architectural programmes were possible until the middle of the century. Most of the construction work was devoted to elegant hôtels owned by the nobility, the majority of which were built in the new suburb of St-Germain. This is also where the *style rocaille*, or rococo style – named after its lively and imaginative shell ornamentation – first developed. Painting in the 17th century was typified by the lofty idealism of Poussin or Claude Lorrain, but in the salons people preferred the scantily-clad frivolity of Boucher or Fragonard. The most important artist of the period was the shy and misanthropic painter Watteau.

In the second half of the century J-A Gabriel's plans for the Place de la Concorde revealed neoclassical tendencies, as did Jacque-Germain Soufflot's ambitious Church of Ste-Geneviève (now the Panthéon).

The storming of the Bastille in 1789 marked not only the end of the *ancien régime*, but the destruction of many church buildings during the years of revolution.

The 19th century

Despite all the changes, Napoleon continued the tradition of the Royal Axis, renaming it the Voie Triomphale (Triumphal Way) and extending it by adding the mighty Arc de Triomphe.

Arc de Triomphe

While most architectural activity during the Restoration was devoted to rebuilding what had been destroyed during the revolutionary years, a combination of neglect and incredibly rapid urban growth – one million inhabitants in 1850, two million in 1870 – had made Paris more than ripe for redevelopment. This finally took place under Napoleon III (1852–70) and his Prefect Georges Haussmann. The dilapidated residential quarter of the Cité was completely pulled down, the existing street system was widened considerably to make room for the large boulevards, and parks were laid out on the outskirts of the city. Garnier's Opéra (1860–75) is a magnificent example of bourgeois *deuxième empire* architecture. Victor Baltard's Halles Centrales – Paris' earliest example of modern iron architecture – were built next to it between 1854 and 1866, but were demolished in 1972. Further iron structures were created for the international exhibitions of 1865, 1867, 1878, 1889 and 1900, among them that vast symbol of the new age, the Eiffel Tower (1889).

79

Paris was now the undisputed cultural centre of all Europe. French painting achieved international importance in the last third of the century with Impressionism. Artists such as Manet, Monet and Renoir replaced gloomy traditional painting styles with *plein-air* painting with its emphasis on sunlight and the natural world. Rather than historical themes, the paintings depicted subjects such as pleasant Sunday outings in the country and boat trips and picnics, capturing the present moment.

The new Paris

Urban development stagnated in Paris until the 1960s. That was when the city experienced its great transformation: facades were cleaned, the Métro was modernised and many sections of the old city were torn down. During the 1970s, under Pompidou, new architectural projects included the Centre Pompidou, the Tour Montparnasse and the skyscraper suburbs of La Défense, Front de Seine and Place d'Italie. The first phase of construction on the Forum des Halles was completed, and the Marais underwent redevelopment. Building projects begun under Giscard (La Villette and Orsay) were completed by Mitterrand, and inspired even larger-scale projects: the extension of the Louvre with the glass pyramid in its inner court, the Opéra Bastille, the Grande Arche at La Défense and the Finance Ministry in Bercy. Work has started on a new building to house the French National Library.

Centre Pompidou

Music and Theatre

The Cultural Scene

Whether you like opera, classical, jazz or rock music, you will have little difficulty finding it in Paris – as long as you don't go in August, when the Parisians are on holiday and many of the venues are closed. From the new Opera de Paris Bastille (opened in 1989), with 2,700 seats, to the huge arena at the Palais d'Omnisports and the smaller Olympia, which host international rock, pop and jazz performances, the choice is enormous. And, of course, there are numerous jazz clubs for which the city is famous (*see page 88* for a small selection).

Check in the weekly *Pariscope* or the *L'officiel des Spectacles* for listings of events and venues and up-to-date information. Also look out for music festivals, and for concerts in museums such as the Louvre, the Musée d'Orsay and the Musée de l'Art Moderne; and in churches such as St-Germain-des-Pres, St-Sulpice, La Madelaine, and many more. These concerts are often, but not always, free. For all other venues, it is best to buy tickets direct from the box office, which can be done by post up to two months in advance. It is also useful to know that ticket agents in the FNAC stores (Forum des Halles, 1 Rue Pierre Lescot, and many other branches) accept credit card bookings for concerts.

Concert poster

Concert venues

Some of the concert halls with the best acoustics are:

Salle Pleyel, 252 Rue du Faubourg St-Honoré, tel: 4561 0630 (*Métro Ternes*).

Salle Gaveau, 45 Rue de la Boétie, tel: 4953 0507 (*Métro Miromesnil*).

Radio-France, 116 Avenue du Président Kennedy, tel: 4230 1516 (*RER Kennedy-Radio France*).

Théâtre des Champs-Elysées, 15 Avenue Montaigne, tel: 4952 5050 (*Métro Franklin-Roosevelt*).

Théâtre de la Ville, Place du Châtelet, tel: 4274 2277 (*Métro Châtelet*).

Théâtre du Châtalet, 2 Rue Edouard-Colonne, tel: 4028 2840 (*Métro Châtalet*)

Auditorium des Halles, Forum des Halles, Porte St-Eustache, tel: 4236 1390 (*Métro Châtelet-Les Halles*).

Theatres

There are around 200 theatre performances in Paris to choose from every single day. Venues range from the Comédie Française, the oldest national theatre in the world, to a host of small independent theatres, where contemporary, sometimes experimental, works are performed, and the *café théâtres*, where new talent can be spotted.

Evening performances usually start between 8.30pm and 9pm. During *Les Grandes Vacances* in August the national theatres are closed (*relâche*). Theatre box offices are usually open from 11am–6pm, and tickets can also be obtained from theatre agents, most of whom accept credit cards, which is not always the case at box offices. The reception desks of most large hotels can also arrange tickets, but usually at a higher price.

Good places to buy tickets are the Kiosque-Théâtre at the Madeleine, *Métro Madeleine*, and in the RER station Châtelet-Les Halles, where, from 12.30–7.30pm from Tuesday to Saturday, leftover tickets for shows are available at half price.

Opera and ballet

Opéra de la Bastille, 120 Rue de Lyon, tel: 4473 1300 (*Métro Bastille*).

Opéra de Paris Garnier, Place de l'Opéra, tel: 4742 5371. Ballet performances only, including modern dance. (*Métro Opéra*).

Opéra Comique, 5 Rue Favart, tel: 4286 8883 (*Métro Richelieu-Drouot*).

Théâtre des Champs Elysées, 15 ave. Montaigne, tel: 4952 5050 (*Métro Franklin-Roosevelt*)

Classical theatre

Comédie Française, Place du Théâtre Français, tel: 4015 0010 (*Métro Palais-Royal*).

Théâtre de l'Europe (Odéon), 1 Place Paul Claudel, tel: 4441 3636 (*Métro Odéon*).

Théâtre National Chaillot, Palais Chaillot, Place du Trocadéro, tel: 4727 8115 (*Métro Trocadéro*).

Modern theatre

Antoine-Simone Berriau, 14 Boulevard de Strasbourg, tel: 4208 7771 (*Métro Strasbourg St Denis*)

Atelier, Place Charles Dullin, tel: 4606 4924 (Métro Anvers).

Bouffes–du-Nord, 37 bis Boulevard de la Chapelle, tel: 4607 3450 (*Métro La Chapelle*)

Oeuvre, 55 Rue de Clichy, tel: 4874 4252 (Métro Clichy).

Théâtre National de la Colline, 15, Rue Malte-Brun, tel: 4366 4360 (*Métro Gambetta*).

Boulevard theatre (comedy)

Théâtre des Bouffes Parisiens, 4 Rue Monsigny, tel: 4296 6024 (*Métro Quatre Septembre*).

Théâtre des Variétés, 7 Boulevard Montmartre, tel: 4233 0992 (*Métro Rue Montmartre*).

Comédie des Champs-Elysées, 15 Avenue Montaigne, tel: 4720 0824 (*Métro Franklin Roosevelt*).

Comédie Française, bust of Molière

Théâtre National Chaillot

Food and Drink

Although Paris is regarded by the French as the gastronomic capital of the country, it still does not possess its own specific Parisian cuisine.

Breakfast *(petit déjeuner)* usually consists of nothing more than a cup of coffee with milk *(café crème)* with a *croissant*, but lunch *(déjeuner)* and dinner *(dîner)* are both very substantial meals. A small hot meal after a visit to the theatre *(souper)* is also quite common.

French cuisine

Particularly good hors d'oeuvres include mushroom salad, egg mayonnaise *(oeuf à la mayonnaise)*, smoked salmon *(saumon fumé)* or a slice of melon with ham *(melon au jambon)*. Specialities include goose-liver paté *(pâté de foie gras)*, duck paté *(terrine de canard)* and sweetbreads with truffles *(timbale de riz de veau)*. All kinds of terrine are highly recommended because they are usually the chef's personal recipes.

Most restaurants serve soup *(soupe)* only in the evening. Two distinctive specialities of French cuisine are snails *(escargots)* and frog's legs *(cuisses de grenouille sautées)*; oysters *(huîtres)* are treated as a normal course and not as a special luxury.

There is a large variety of fish and seafood – not only confined to specialist restaurants. Flounder *(butte)* and angler *(lotte)* are particularly delicious.

83

Seafood platter

Where meat is concerned there is a choice of mutton *(mouton)*, lamb *(agneau)*, beef *(boeuf)* and pork *(porc)*. It is usually either served fried *(rôti)* or boiled *(natur, bouilli)*.

A selection of cheeses *(fromages)* is an integral part of any French meal.

Recommended desserts – alongside the classic *mousse au chocolat* – include ice cream floating in vanilla sauce *(île flottante)* as well as a variety of home-made cakes and tarts *(tarte maison)*.

Drinks

A French meal is usually accompanied by a glass *(un verre)* of white or red wine *(vin blanc, vin rouge)*. The rosé wine is also excellent. In good restaurants it is always a good idea to follow the recommendation of the manager or his staff. The French are also drinking more and more beer *(bière)* these days. Another typical drink is the *apéritif*, usually consumed in corner bistros.

Waiting for his tip

Restaurants

Restaurants in France are required by law to display their menu outside the entrance, showing the current prices

Bell boys at the Fouquet

which usually include service (service compris). Bread is served at all meals free of charge.

The following list can only serve as the roughest of guides. The restaurants have been subdivided into four categories: $$$$ = luxury, $$$ = expensive, $$ = moderately priced, $ = inexpensive.

$$$$: **La Tour d'Argent**, 15 Quai de la Tournelle; **Maxim's**, 3 Rue Royale; **Ambroisie**, 9 Place des Vosges; **Jacques Cagna**, 14 Rue des Grands Augustins, **Fouquet**, 99 Ave des Champs Elysées.

$$$: **Le Grand Café**, 4 Boulevard des Capuchines; **La Terrasse**, 2 Place de l'Ecole Militaire; **Le Beauvilliers**, 52 Rue Lamarck; **Le Train Bleu**, 20 Boulevard Diderot (in the Gare de Lyon); **Brasserie Lipp**, 151 Boulevard St-Germain; **Coconnas**, 2 bis Place des Vosges.

$$: **Au Pied de Cochon**, 6 Rue Coquillière; **Chez Flo**, 7 Cour des Petites Ecuries; **Vagenende**, 142 Boulevard St-Germain; **La Fermette Marbeuf**, 5 Rue Marbeuf; **Au Petit Riche**, 25 Rue Le Peletiers; **Bofinger**, 5 Rue de la Bastille; **La Coupole**, 102 Boulevard du Montparnasse; **Le Boeuf sur le Toit**, 34 Rue du Colisée.

$: **Le Zephyr**, 1 Rue Jourdain; **Le Durer**, 19 Rue Yvonne le Tac; **Chartier**, 7 Rue du Faubourg Montmartre; **Les Caves du Marais**, 5 Rue Caron; **Sans Culottes**, 9 Rue Guisard; **L'Arbre à Canelle**, 57 Passage des Panoramas.

Bistros

The small café-bar on almost every street corner in Paris usually styles itself as a bar or brasserie, and sometimes even as a café, but the French refer to all these establishments as bistros. They provide breakfast, simple morning and evening snacks, and all kinds of alcoholic and non-alcoholic drinks.

Enjoying a beer

Shopping

Parisian refinement...

Among the most attractive places to shop in Paris are the city's old arcades, which have recently been restored true to their original style.

...elegance

Passage du Caire: 234 Rue St-Denis, *Métro Sentier*; Passage du Panorama, 11 Blvd Montmartre, *Métro Rue Montmartre*; Galerie Vivienne, 4 Rue des Petits-Champs, *Métro Bourse*.

Department stores

Au Printemps, 64 Boulevard Haussmann, *Métro Havre-Caumartin*; Galeries Lafayette, 40 Boulevard Haussmann, *Métro Chaussée d'Antin*, and also 22 Rue du Départ, *Métro Montparnasse-Bienvenue*; La Samaritaine, 75 Rue de Rivoli, *Métro Châtelet*; Bazar de l'Hôtel de Ville, 50 Rue de Rivoli, *Métro Hôtel de Ville*; Au Bon Marché, 135 Rue du Bac, *Métro Sèvres-Babylon*; La Belle Jardinière, 2 Rue du Pont Neuf, *Métro Pont Neuf*; Les Trois Quartiers, 17 Boulevard de la Madeleine, *Métro Madeleine*; Virgin (CDs, and records), 60 Avenue des Champs-Elysées.

Fashion

Haute couture shows are held in January and June, and almost all the main fashion giants have branches around the Champs-Elysées, especially in the Avenue Montaigne, *Métro Alma-Marceau* and *F D Roosevelt*, in the Avenue George V, *Métro George V*, and also in the Rue du Faubourg St-Honoré between Rue Royale, *Métro Madeleine*, and the church of St-Philippe-en-Roule, *Métro St-Philippe-en-Roule*.

...and chic

A new centre, mostly featuring younger fashion designers, is around the Place des Victoires, *Métro Bourse*: Kenzo, 3 Place des Victoires, and Jean-Paul Gaultier, 70 Rue Vivienne.

Men's fashion, off-the-peg but expensive, can be found at Armani, Cardin, Yves St Laurent, and other outlets on the Right Bank, while Yamamoto and Versace designs are sold in Left Bank boutiques.

Haute Couture that isn't totally up-to-date gets sold off relatively cheaply in the so-called *Dégriffés* shops. Most can be found in the Rue St-Placide, *Métro St-Placide*, and in the Rue Alésia, *Métro Alésia*.

Teenage fashion is mostly to be found in the Rue de la Chaussée d'Antin, *Métro Chaussée d'Antin*, in the area around Maine-Montparnasse and in the Quartier Latin (Blvd St-Michel).

Out shopping

Perfumes

Alongside the city's innumerable parfumeries and the huge perfume departments of the major stores there are also a few firms that sell their own products exclusively.

Marcel Guerlain, 2 Place Vendôme, *Métro Tuileries*; 29 Rue de Sèvres, *Métro Sèvres-Babylone*; 68 Avenue des Champs-Elysées, *Métro George V*; Marcel Rochas, 33 Rue François Ier, *Métro George V*; Roger et Gallet, 62 Rue du Faubourg St-Honoré, *Métro Concorde*.

Markets

Flowers: Place de la République, *Métro République*, daily except Monday 9am–7.30pm; Place Louis-Lépine, *Métro Cité*, daily except Sunday and public holidays 8am–7pm; Place de la Madeleine, *Métro Madeleine*, Tuesday, Wednesday, Friday, Saturday and also on the eve of public holidays 9am–7.30pm; Place des Ternes, *Métro Ternes*, Tuesday, Wednesday, Friday and Saturday and also on the eve of public holidays 9am–7.30pm.

Fabrics: Marché Saint-Pierre, Place Saint-Pierre, *Métro Anvers*, except Sunday.

Birds: Marché aux Oiseaux, Place Louis-Lépine, *Métro Cité*, every Sunday 9am–7pm; Quai de la Mégisserie, *Métro Châtelet* or *Pont Neuf*, daily except Sunday, 9am–7pm.

Thinking pink

Flea markets: Marché aux Puces de St-Ouen, Rue des Rosiers, St-Ouen, *Métro Porte de Clignancourt*. The biggest and best known one, though the selection has become extremely patchy in recent years. Saturday (best day), Sunday and Monday; Marché aux Puces, Porte de Montreuil, *Métro Porte de Montreuil*, Saturday and Sunday 8am–8pm, Monday morning.

Bric-a-brac/antiques: Carreau du Temple, 1 Rue Dupetit-Thouars, *Métro République*, daily 9am–noon, Monday 9am–7pm; Marché d'Aligre, Place d'Aligre, *Métro Ledru-Rollin*, daily market until noon, clothing and flea market, 10am–7pm; Ave Georges-Lafenestre, *Métro Porte de Vanves*, Saturday and Sunday, 8am–6.30pm.

Nightlife

Paris is a city that never sleeps. There's always something going on whatever time it is. Lists of events can either be found in the daily papers or in the city's 'What's On' guides called *Officiel des Spectacles* and *Pariscope*, published every Wednesday. The following is a brief selection.

Cabarets

The cabarets and major revue theatres in Paris usually do two shows a night, and three at weekends. With the big shows, the so-called *dîner-spectacle* usually begins at 8pm, and the evening meal is generally included in the price, which varies but is never cheap. The 'Champagne Shows' – at which a half-bottle of expensive champagne is provided – start at 10pm and midnight.

The cabaret theatres include the three most famous ones: The **Folies Bergères**, the oldest in Paris, the **Lido**, where the Bluebell Girls perform, and the **Moulin-Rouge**, immortalised by Toulouse-Lautrec. The list below gives details of these and other venues.

Ane Rouge, 3 Rue Langier, tel: 4562 5242 (*Métro Ternes*). Dîner-spectacle from 8pm.

Crazy Horse Saloon, 12 Avenue George V, tel: 4723 3232 (*Métro George V*). Shows begin 8.45pm and 11.15pm, Friday and Saturday 10.30pm and 12.50am.

Don Camillo, 10 Rue des Saints-Pères, tel: 4260 8284 (*Métro St-Germain-des-Prés*). Shows begin at 8pm.

Elephant Bleu, 49 Rue de Ponthieu, tel: 4359 5864 (*Métro George V*). Dinner at 8pm; show at 10pm.

Folies-Bergères, 32 Rue Richer, tel: 4246 7711 (*Métro Cadet*). Performances begin 8pm, 10pm and midnight.

Illuminated fountain on Place Colette

Paris by night

Lido, 116 Avenue des Champs-Elysées, tel: 4076 5610 (*Métro Place Charles-de-Gaulle/Etoile* or *George V*). Performances begin 8pm, 10pm and midnight.

Michou, 80 Rue des Martyrs, tel: 4606 1604 (*Métro Pigalle* or *Blanche*). Drag show with dinner from 9pm.

Moulin Rouge, Place Blanche, tel: 4606 0019, (*Métro Blanche*). Performances start at 8pm, 10pm and midnight.

Paradis Latin, 28 Rue du Cardinal-Lemoine, tel: 4329 0707 (*Métro Cardinal-Lemoine*). 'Dinner-Revue' at 8pm, 'Champagne Show' at 10pm, except Tuesday.

Rôtisserie de l'Abbaye, 22 Rue Jacob, tel: 4562 6804 (*Métro St-Germain-des-Prés*). Dîner -spectacle in a typical 13th-century cellar.

Cabaret singers

Caveau des Oubliettes, 11 Rue St-Julien-le-Pauvre (*Métro St-Michel*). From 9pm, except Monday.

Deux Anes, 100 Boulevard de Clichy (*Métro Blanche*).

Lapin Agile, 22 Rue des Saules (*Métro Lamarck-Caulaincourt*). From 9pm, except Monday.

Discotheques

Rive droite:

Balajo, 99 Rue de la Lappe, trendy (*Métro Bastille*).

Les Bains, 7 Rue du Bourg-l'Abbé, full of theatrical and fashion people (*Métro Etienne-Marcel*).

Bus Palladium, 6 Rue Fontaine (*Métro Blanche*).

Castel's, 15 Rue Princesse (*Métro San Germaine*).

Chalet du Lac, Orée du Bois de Vincennes (*Métro St-Mandé-Tourelles*).

La Locomotive, 9 Bd. de Clichy (*Métro Blanche*).

La Main Jaune, Place de la Porte Champerret (for roller-skate acrobats) (*Métro Porte Champerret*).

Le Palace, 8 Rue Faubourg Montmartre (*Métro Rue Montmartre*).

La Scala, 188 bis Rue de Rivoli (*Métro Palais-Royal*).

Blowing up a storm

Rive gauche:

Chez Felix (samba orchestra), 23 Rue Mouffetard (*Métro Monge*).

New Riverside, 7 Rue Grégoire de Tours (*Métro Odéon*).

Le Tabou, 33 Rue Dauphine (*Métro Odéon*).

Duc des Lombards, 42 Rue des Lombards (*Métro les Halles*).

Latitudes St-Germain, 7-11 Rue St-Benoît (*Métro St-Germain-des-Prés*).

Zed Club, 2 Rue des Anglais (*Métro Maubert-Mutualité*).

Jazz clubs

The best place to enjoy the jazz scene on the rive droite is to stroll along the Rue des Lombards, Métro Châtelet,

Welcome to the club

and on the rive gauche the Rue St-Benoît, Métro St-Germain-des-Prés; both streets contain several jazz clubs and pubs. Other recommended clubs include:

Le Caveau de la Huchette, 5 Rue de la Huchette (*Métro St-Michel*).

New Morning, 7–9 Rue des Petites Ecuries (*Métro Château d'Eau*).

Nightclubs

In the area around the Forum des Halles and also between Place Blanche and Place Pigalle there are numerous clubs offering what they call a 'Parisian atmosphere' with striptease performances.

As in many other capital cities, a lot of these establishments are clip-joints, and however 'charming' the service might be it is a good idea to avoid ordering too much. Also, avoid the smaller, lesser-known places. They are not likely to be more 'authentic' or interesting, but may well be very sleazy.

The following clubs, though not cheap, still have relatively good reputations:

Capricorne, 5 Rue Molière, tel: 4296 2027 (*Métro Palais-Royal*).

Les 2 Boules, 28 Rue des Ecoles, tel: 4046 9699 (*Métro Odéon*).

Show Girls, 5 Rue des Halles, tel: 4233 8588 (*Métro Châtelet-Les Halles*).

Chez Moune, 54 Rue Pigalle, tel: 4526 6464 (*Métro Pigalle*).

The cabarets on the Butte Montmartre have a lot more atmosphere and have the added attraction of being in a picturesque part of the city. This same *ambiance* can also be found around the Gare Montparnasse.

Getting There

By Air

Air France is the main agent for all flights to France from America and from other European countries. Each of Paris' airports has two terminals, connected by buses that run free of charge. Also free are the bus connections between the respective RER terminals and the actual air terminals. An automatic train, Orlyval, runs between the two airports roughly every 5 minutes from 5.50am to 11.45pm.

Roissy-Charles-de-Gaulle Airport (23km/15 miles north of Paris):

To get there: Air France Bus, leaves every 15 minutes, 5.45am–11pm from Terminal Porte-Maillot and Place de L'Etoile (Avenue Carnot); hourly connections from 7am–9pm from Gare Montparnasse (bus stop is at 13 Boulevard de Vaugirard).

Roissy-Rail (*RER line B3*), departs every 15 minutes 5.30am–11.30pm from city centre.

Buses: No 350 from Gare de l'Est, Gare du Nord, Porte de la Chapelle, Le Bourget, or bus No 351 from Place de la Nation. The Roissy-Bus also departs every 15 minutes between the airport and the Old Opera House (corner of Rue Scribe/Rue Aubert).

Orly Airport (14km/9 miles south of Paris):

To get there: Air France Bus, departs every 15 minutes, 6am–11pm, from Terminal Invalides (with a further stop at *Gare Montparnasse*).

Orly-Rail (*RER line C2*), departs every 15 minutes 5.30am–11pm from the city centre as far as Pont de Rungis station; the journey continues by bus or the *RER line B4* to Antony, and from there with the fully automatic Métro Orly-Val to the airport.

Buses: Orly Bus from Denfert-Rochereau.

By Train

Paris can be reached by train from all over continental Europe. There are six railway stations and each one is on at least two Métro or RER lines. The name of the Métro stop is the same as the station. There are baggage check counters (*consigne*) and coin-operated lockers (*consigne automatique*) at every station.

Tickets may be booked for through journeys from the UK, including ferry travel, from any British Rail station; BR travel centres can supply details of continental services, or contact British Rail International Enquiries, Victoria Station, London SW1, tel: 071-834 2345.

Some passengers can obtain discounted fares, eg young people under 26 can buy cheap return tickets to Paris and holders of a senior citizen's rail passes can pay a small extra sum for a Rail Europe card which then entitles them

Discussing departures

to a 50 percent reduction on fares; a Family Rail Europe card is also available for family groups of a minimum of three and maximum of eight people, which can be used to purchase cheaper tickets. Details of these deals can be obtained from the International Rail Centre at Victoria. Eurotrain, tel: 0171-730 3402 also offers 30 percent of standard two-month return tickets for those under 26.

Channel Tunnel: The Channel Tunnel, which opened at the end of 1994, offers a 35-minute drive-on rail service under the Channel between London and Paris (total journey time is about three hours). For infomation/reservations, tel: 01303 271100.

By Car

Parking meter

A car should really only be used for arrival and departure, because Paris traffic can be very tricky. It's also almost impossible to find anywhere to park.

The fastest highways to Paris are the *autoroutes*, toll roads run by private companies. There are service stations every 25km (15 miles) or so, with petrol, food, coffee and restrooms, generally open 24 hours a day. At the border, there are no special formalities for cars entering France for less than six months, but you will have to show proof of insurance, and it is wise, though not obligatory, to have international green card insurance, obtainable from your own insurance company.

Speed limits: Maximum speeds permitted: on motorways 130kmph (80mph), on main roads 110kmph (68mph), on country roads 90kmph (55mph) and in built-up areas 50kmph (30mph).

Breakdown service: Breakdown and tow-away services in France are well organised. Help can be obtained on motorways via the emergency telephone, and from the emergency *Police Secours* number (dial 17) on country roads and in towns and villages.

Documentation: Motorists need their car papers, driving licence and nationality sticker.

By Coach

Eurolines, a consortium of almost 30 coach companies, operates daily services from London Victoria to Paris. One of the cheapest ways of reaching the city, discounts are available for young people and senior citizens. The ticket includes the ferry crossing (via Dover) and National Express coaches have connections with the London departures from most major towns in the UK.

For details contact Eurolines UK, 52 Grosvenor Gardens, Victoria, London SW1W 0AU, tel: 0171-730 0202; or in France at the Gare Routière Internationale, 3-5 Avenue de la Porte-de-la-Villette, 75019 Paris, tel: (1) 4038 9393, fax: (1) 4035 0131.

Getting Around

Métro

At the beginning of the century the Métro consisted of various different sections. Today the 200-km (125-mile) long rail network has 367 stations, and is being continually extended in the suburban areas. Fifteen different Métro lines cross the city.

The Métro and the RER

During peak traffic hours, there is up to one train a minute. The tickets are valid for the entire Métro network, allowing passengers to travel as far as they like and change as often as they wish.

Before travelling it is a good idea to purchase a *carnet* of 10 single tickets, which costs less. Machines at the entry to the Métro punch the tickets automatically.

For week-long stays, one should purchase the *coupon jaune hebdomadaire* (remember to bring along a passport-sized photo). This ticket is valid Monday to Sunday on all Métro, RER and bus lines within the city limits.

Those wishing to travel a lot, but who are only in Paris for a few days, should certainly buy a tourist ticket (*Formule 1* and *Paris-Visite*), valid for 1, 3 or 5 days.

The first Métro train runs at 5.30am, the last leaves at around 12.30am.

RER (Réseau Express Régional)

The lines of the RER (the so-called Express Métro) are not only useful for those wishing to cross the city in a hurry, but also for excursions into the surrounding Ile de France and to the airports. There are four lines, A, B, C and D, and for clearer identification the RER trains also have names. The trains run underground in the city centre, and above ground in the suburban areas.

Within the city, Métro tickets are also valid for the RER (first and second class).

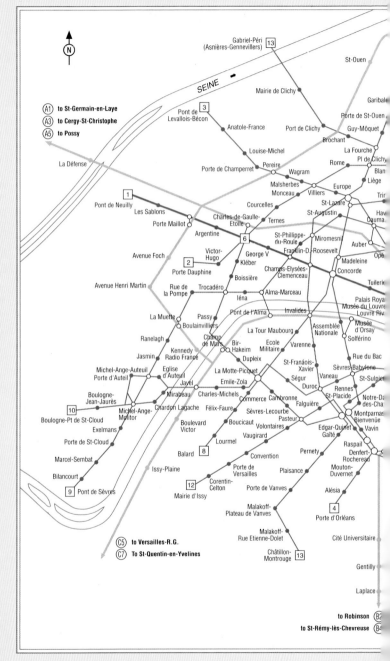

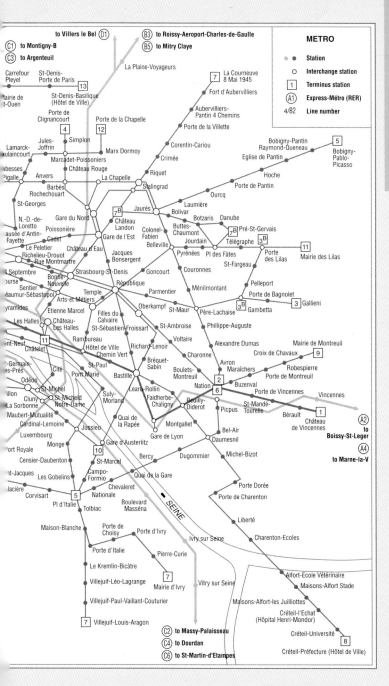

METRO

- Station
- Interchange station
- Terminus station
- Express-Métro (RER)
- Line number

Buses

Bus stops have a recognisable red-and-yellow sign, bearing the numbers of the various lines. The bus lines with numbers on a white background run daily, and those on a black background Monday–Saturday only.

Buses run from 7am–8.30pm, with only a few lines continuing until 12.30am.

Taking a bus during rush hour usually isn't a good idea because of the endless queues.

Night buses: Night buses connect the Place du Châtelet with the city limits.

Departures from the Place du Châtelet are hourly from 1.30am–5.30am, and 1am–5am in the other direction. The lines are:

A: Châtelet – Louvre – Concorde – Place Charles-de-Gaulle/Etoile – Pont de Neuilly – La Défense.

B: Châtelet – Louvre – Opéra – St-Lazare – Levallois.

C: Châtelet – Louvre – Pigalle – Clichy (Mairie).

D: Châtelet – Louvre – Gare du Nord – Porte de Clignancourt – St-Ouen (Mairie).

E: Châtelet – Gare de L'Est – Pantin.

F: Châtelet – République – Belleville – Les Lilas.

G: Châtelet – République – Père-Lachaise – Montreuil.

H: Châtelet – Bastille – Nation – Vincennes.

J: Châtelet – Sorbonne – Boulevard St-Michel – Porte d'Orlèans.

R: Châtelet – Place d'Italie – Marché de Rungis.

Sightseeing by bus

City sightseeing tours by scheduled bus

Recommended lines for your own individual sightseeing tours by scheduled bus are the following: 24, 29, 30, 32, 38, 42, 63, 69, 85.

A friendly taxi-driver

Taxis

During the day, unoccupied taxis can be recognised by their illuminated white roof-signs, showing Tarif A (Paris). At night and also on Sundays and weekends they drive with orange signs, showing the Tarif B.

Radio taxis can be reached at the following numbers (be prepared to wait a while during rush hour) tel: 4739 3333, 4936 1010, 4585 8585, 4270 0042. Remember that these cabs include the distance driven to reach customers and also waiting time in their overall fares.

Bicycle hire

Information and hire: Paris-Vélo, 2 Rue du Fer-à-Moulin, 75005 Paris, tel: 4337 5922, fax: 4707 6745; Bicy-Club. 8 Porte des Champerret, tel: 4766 5592 (six different outlets in and around Paris).

It is sometimes possible to rent bicycles from RER stations and some Métro stations at the weekend.

Facts for the Visitor

Travel times

The best times to travel to Paris are spring and autumn. During summer (mid-July until the end of August) the city is very quiet. The period leading up to Christmas is also recommended; the best artistic and cultural events of the year generally take place in November and December.

Just arrived

Travel documents

All visitors to France need a valid passport. No visa is currently required by visitors from any EU country, or from the US, Canada, New Zealand or Japan. Nationals of other countries do require a visa. If you intend to stay in France for more than 90 days at any one time, then a *carte de séjour* must be obtained from the French consulate – this also applies to EU members until restrictions are relaxed.

Customs

Non-EU members can bring 400 cigarettes, one bottle of spirits, two of wine and 50g of perfume. EU-members have guide levels of 800 cigarettes, 10 litres of spirit and 90 litres of wine. Customs keep a close watch for drugs, which are illegal.

97

Foreign exchange

There is no limit on the amount of money that may be taken in or out of the country, but sums amounting to more than FF50,000 in equivalent value must be declared.

Tourist Information Offices

Tourist information

Information and brochures are available from French tourist information offices but they do not make hotel reservations.

French Government Tourist Office, 178 Piccadilly, London W1V 0AL, tel: 0171-499 6911, fax: 0171-493 6594.

French Government Tourist Office, 610 Fifth Avenue, Suite 222, New York, NY 10020-2452, tel: 212-757 1125, fax: 212-247 6468; 9454 Wilshire Boulevard, Beverley Hills, Los Angeles, CA 90212-2967, tel: 213-272 2661; 645 North Michigan Avenue, Suite 630, Chicago, Illinois 60611-2836, tel: 312-337 6301; Cedar Maple Plaza, 2305 Cedar Springs Road, Suite 205, Dallas, Texas 75201, tel: 214-720 4010, fax: 214-702 0250.

French Government Tourist Office, 1981 McGill College, Tour Esso, Suite 490, Montreal H3A 2W9, Quebec, tel: 514-288 4264, fax: 514-845 4868; 30 St Patrick Street, Suite 700, Toronto M5T 3A3 Ontario, tel: 416-593 6427.

In Paris, information may be obtained from the Office de Tourisme de Paris, 127 Avenue des Champs-Elysées, 75008 Paris, tel: 4952 5354.

'What's On' guides

The weekly publications *Pariscope – Une Semaine à Paris*, *L'Officiel des Spectacles*, and *7 à Paris* contain details of events taking place in and around Paris.

Sightseeing

Sightseeing tours are provided by the following organisations:

Bus tours

Paris-Vision, 214 Rue de Rivoli, Métro Tuileries.
Cityrama-Rapid Pullman, 4 Place des Pyramides, Métro Tuileries.

Excursions Parisiennes: Hotels look after the bookings and collection points.

Rail Tours

SNCF (French national railway), 16 Boulevard des Capucines. Information in English, tel: 4582 0841.

RATP (Paris transport authority), Place de la Madeleine.

Seine boats

Seeing the city from the Seine

Sightseeing trips by boat along the Seine are provided by several organisations. They generally take 1½ hours, or 3 hours including lunch or dinner. The ships run all year round; every half-hour between April and October, 9.30am–11pm. Board at: Pont de L'Alma (right bank) for *Bateaux Mouches*, the Pont Neuf for *Vedettes du Pont Neuf* and at the Eiffel Tower for *Bateaux Parisiens*.

The *Batobus* also plies the Seine approximately every 30 minutes between May and September, 10am–7pm. There are several boarding points and passengers may embark and disembark where they like, having purchased a day ticket.

Canauxrama (tel: 4239 1500) and *Paris-Canal* (tel: 4240 9697) also offer trips along the city's canals and in the surrounding area. For more information, look under '*A travers Paris*' in the 'What's On' guides.

City tours

The following organisations can provide multilingual hostesses on request and arrange sightseeing tours for individuals or groups on various themes:

Union Centrale des Arts Décoratifs, 107 Rue de Rivoli, F-75001 Paris, tel: 4260 3214, App. 26 (2–6pm).

Caisse Nationale des Monuments Historiques, 62 Rue St-Antoine, F-75004 Paris, tel: 4461 2169 or 4461 2000.

Musées de France, Bureau de l'Action Culturelle, 9 Quai Anatole France, F-75007 Paris, tel: 4296 5830.

The *Office de Tourisme de Paris* (*see page 97*) can also provide interpreters.

Views

The best panoramic views of Paris can be had from the observation platform of the Eiffel Tower, from the top of the Arc de Triomphe in the Place de l'Etoile, from the terrace of the Sacré-Coeur, from the towers of Notre-Dame, from the top of the Samaritaine department store and also from the Tour Montparnasse.

View from Sacré Coeur

Money

The unit of currency in France is the French franc (FF), divided into 100 *centimes* (c). In circulation are 10, 5, 2 and 1-franc coins, and 50, 20, 10 and 5-centime coins. Banknotes are issued for 500, 200, 100, 50 and 20 francs.

Banks and exchange

Banks are open Monday to Friday 9am–noon and 2pm–4pm (often closed during the afternoon on days preceding public holidays).

Twenty-four hour money exchange at Orly and Roissy airports. Bank counters in SCNF rail stations are open until 10pm on weekdays. (Gare du Nord until 9pm, Gare de Lyon until 11pm). Money can be exchanged until 7pm on Sunday at the Gare Montparnasse. Some branches of the CCF have extended opening hours: 115 Champs-Elysées (daily 8.30am–8pm); 2 Carrefour de l'Odéon (Monday to Saturday 9am–7.30pm). There is also an automatic money-changer for sterling, D-Marks, and Italian lire outside the BRED branch at 66 Champs-Elysées.

Current exchange rates can be found in newspapers or at banks. Cheques may be cashed up to a limit of FF1,400.

Opening hours

Shops: Opening hours for shops in France tend to vary a lot, except for department stores. Generally speaking, shops are open until 7pm, and on weekdays supermarkets sometimes stay open until 11pm.

Government agencies: Monday to Friday, 9am–noon and 2–5pm.

Museums

Museums in Paris are usually closed on Monday and Tuesday. Because of the huge crush to get into some museums and special exhibitions, the *Réunion des Musées Nationaux* has opened a shop in which museum tickets can be ordered and bought in advance in France or from abroad: Musées & Compagnie, 49 Rue Etienne-Marcel, tel: 4013 4913.

Cartes Inter-Musées are passes allowing access to over 80 museums and sights in Paris, obtainable at the larger Métro stations, the Office de Tourisme (*see page 97*) and at *Musées & Compagnie*.

Postal services

The French post office is run by the PTT *Poste et Télécommunications*, and although delivery may be prompt and efficient, customer services are not; unless you arrive at a quiet time in an out of the way bureau, be prepared to wait. Fortunately there are many *bureaux de postes* around the city – each marked by a stylised blue aeroplane on a yellow sign – where you can consult the phone book (*bottin*), buy telephone cards, send or receive money orders (*mandats*), call anywhere in the world, and of course, mail a letter (look for the counter marked *affranchissement*, *timbres*, or *poste aérienne*). Most branches are open Monday to Friday 8am–7pm, and Saturday 8am–noon. All general delivery, if not otherwise specified, is sent to the main post office at 52 Rue du Louvre, 75001, tel: 4233 7160, Métro Louvre. The Post Office is open 24 hours a day for telephone and telegraphs and until 7pm for other services.

You can also drop your letters into the distinctive yellow mail boxes, often located at *tabacs* (tobacco stores) where they sell stamps as well. To send a telegram in English, tel: 4233 2111.

PTT post offices are open Monday to Friday, 8am–7pm, Saturday until noon.

The central post office, 52 Rue du Louvre, Métro Louvre, is open all night; the Elysées post office, 71 Avenue des Champs-Elysées, from 8am–11pm.

Phoning home

Telephone

Foreign calls are half-price after 9.30pm. They can also be made from any public telephone box (*cabines publiques*). The dialling code for all countries is 19, then wait for the second bleep. Then dial the country code required – Australia 61; Germany 49; Italy 39; Japan 81; Netherlands 31; Spain 34; United Kingdom 44; US and Canada 1. AT&T: 19 0011; Sprint: 19 0087.

Most public phones in Paris can only be operated with *Télécartes* (which come in 50 and 120-unit versions). They can be purchased at post offices, Métro ticket counters and tobacconists. For other phone boxes, 50-centime, 1-franc or 5-franc coins are required. Phone calls can be made from most cafés without the need to buy anything to eat or drink. All phone boxes can be rung back. The number can be found on the small sign in the box with the blue bell.

The dialling code to reach France from abroad is 33, and for Paris 331.

Enquiries: inland, dial 12; operator services, 13.

Time

France is six hours ahead of US Eastern Standard Time and one ahead of Greenwich Mean Time.

Voltage

220 volts AC, though 110 still exists in rare cases. An adapter for two-point sockets is needed.

Public holidays

1 January, Easter Monday, 1 May, 8 May (1945 Armistice), Ascension, Whit Monday, 14 July (national holiday), 15 August, 1 November, 11 November (1918 Armistice), Christmas Day.

Medical assistance

Visitors from the EU have the right to claim the same health services available to the French. UK visitors should obtain form E111 from the Department of Health prior to departure. It is still advisable to have private health insurance in case of circumstances not covered by the reciprocal arrangement.

For visitors from outside the EU, also, the best way to guarantee problem-free medical treatment is to take out a private traveller's health insurance policy. Information from travel agents and health insurance companies.

Emergencies: Police 17, Fire Brigade 18, Ambulance 4378 2626, Emergency Doctor 4707 7777.

Hospital entrance

Keeping a watchful eye

101

Drinking water

Although tap-water in Paris can be drunk, mineral water is preferable and tastes better.

Toilets

The city has replaced the old public lavatories *(pissoirs)* with modern *Sanisettes*. These cost FF2 per visit, but are chemically cleaned and even have music. Lavatories in restaurants and bistros may be used free of charge, and there is no need to buy anything out of politeness. The larger Métro stations also have public conveniences maintained by ladies who expect a tip of about FF2.

Lost property

Bureau des Objets Trouvés, 36 Rue des Morillons, Métro Convention, tel: 4828 3236. Open Monday to Friday 8.30am–5pm, Thursday until 8pm.

Embassies and consulates

American Embassy, 2 Rue St-Florentin, 75001 Paris, tel: (1) 4296 1488.

Australian Embassy, 4 Rue Jean-Rey, 75015 Paris, tel: (1) 4575 6200.

British Embassy, 9 Avenue Hoche, 75008 Paris, tel: (1) 4266 9142.

Canadian Embassy, 35 Avenue Montaigne, 75008 Paris, tel: (1) 4723 0101.

The British Embassy

A shady square

Accommodation

There are around 5,000 hotels in Paris, of which about 1,200 are called Hôtels de Tourisme and are highly recommended. They are regularly checked by the state and can be recognised immediately by their dark-blue, octagonal signs with a white 'H' in the middle, outside their entrances. The stars above the letter denote the category, and the letters NN *(nouvelle norme)* mean that the hotel is up to the very latest tourist standards. The official French classification system has five categories, ranging from no stars to four stars. Since hotels in Paris are at a premium, especially during peak season, it is best to reserve a room directly with a hotel weeks in advance, or else book one of the cheap deals through your travel agent.

Hotel reservation office

Booking a hotel room in advance via the hotel reservation office is only possible on the spot, but it provides the best chances of finding accommodation.

Office de Tourisme de Paris, 127, Avenue des Champs-Elysées, tel: 49525354 *(Métro Charles-de-Gaulle-Etoile)*. Opening hours: daily 9am–8pm.

The following is a very brief selection of recommended hotels ranging from expensive to moderate and inexpensive. The number in brackets refers to the *arrondissement* (*see page 9*). A list of all Hôtels de Tourisme is available from the French Tourist Office (*see page 97*).

$$$$
Hotel Intercontinental, 3 Rue Castiglione (1); **Hôtel de Crillon**, 10 Place de la Concorde (1); **Hôtel Regina**, 2 Place des Pyramides (1); **Hôtel Maurice**, 228 Rue de Rivoli (1).

$$$
Le Colbert, 7 Rue de l'Hôtel Colbert (5); **Familia**, 11, Rue des Ecoles, (5); **Bretonnerie**, 22, Rue Ste-Croix-de-la-Bretonnerie (4); **Hôtel du Jeu de Paume**, 54 Rue St-Louis-en-l'Ile (4); **Hôtel des Marroniers**, 21 Rue Jacob (6).

$$ ~
Champ de Mars, 7 Rue de Champ de Mars (7); **Lecourbe**, 28 Rue Lecourbe (15); **Timhôtel-Montmartre**, 11 Place Emile Goudeau (18).

Young people's hotels and student hostels

The organisation AJF (*Accueil des Jeunes en France*) always guarantees young travellers cheap accommodation.

A brochure listing all the addresses can be obtained from the central reservation office for group and solo travel: Accueil des Jeunes en France-AJF, 119, Rue St-Martin, F-75004 Paris, tel: 42778780 (*Métro Rambuteau/LesHalles/Hôtel de Ville*).

This office and its branches organise accommodation in youth hostels and also in four (recommended) hotels in the 4th *arrondissement* especially for young people.

The branches are at the following addresses: 16 Rue du Pont-Louis-Philippe (4) (*Métro Pont Marie*); 139 Boulevard St-Michel, (5) (*RER Port-Royal*).

Maisons Internationales de la Jeunesse et des Estudiants (MIJE) also provides cheap accommodation for the under 30s. 11, Rue du Fauconnier, tel: 4274 2345.

Addresses: Cité Internationale Universitaire, 19 Bd. Jourdain, F-75014 Paris, tel: 45896852 (*RER Cité Universitaire*).

Youth Hostels: Foreigners need to show their international youth hostel identity card. Stays are limited to a maximum of eight days. There is no age limit imposed at these hostels.

Information available from the *Fédération Unie des Auberges de Jeunesse*, 27 Rue Pajol, F-75018 Paris, tel: 46070001, or from the relevant youth hostelling association in your own country.

Camping

An international camping permit is recommended. Information on campsites can be obtained from the Office de Tourisme, 127 Avenue des Champs-Elysées, F-75008 (*Métro Charles-de-Gaulle-Etoile*).

Campsites: Camping du Bois de Boulogne, Allée du Bord de L'Eau, F-75016 Paris, tel: 45243000. From Métro Porte Maillot take bus No 244 (open all year round). Camping de Versailles, 31 Rue Berethelot, F-78000 Versailles, tel: 39512361 (*RER C5, station Porchefontaine*) Open from Palm Sunday until 31 October.

Index

Académie Française ...**60**
Arc de Triomphe **34–5**
Arc de Triomphe du
  Carroussel **30**
Archives Nationales ...**45**
Arènes de Lutèce........**69**

Banque de France **39**
Bibliothèque
  National **38**
Bois de Boulogne **69**
Bourse **38**
Bourse du
  Commerce **43**

Café Aux Deux
  Magots **59**
Café de Flore **59**
Café de la Paix **37**
Catacombs **68**
Centre International des
  Industries et
  Techniques **70**
Centre National d'Art et
  de Culture (Centre
  Pompidou) **45**
Champ de Mars **63**
Champs Elysées **32**
Churches
  Dôme des
    Invalides................**64**
  Notre-Dame **18–20**
  Sacré Coeur **53–4**
  Saint-Eustache **43**
  Saint-Jean
    l'Evangeliste..........**53**
  Saint-Roch **41**
  Saint-Séverin **55**
  Sainte-Marie
    Madeleine **36**
  St-Gervais-St-
    Protais **47**
  St-Etienne-du-
    Mont........................**58**
  St-Germain-des-
    Prés **59**
  St-Jean-St-François ..**51**
  St-Julien-le-Pauvre ..**56**
  St-Louis des
    Invalides................**65**
  St-Louis en l'Ile.......**21**
  St-Pierre de
    Montmartre **53**
  St-Sulpice **59**
  Ste-Ursule-de-la-
    Sorbonne **57**
  Val-de-Grâce **57**
Cimetière
  Montmartre...............**54**
Cimetière St-Pierre......**53**

Cimetière de
  Montparnasse **68**
Cirque d'Hiver **51**
Cité de la Musique **71**
Colonne de Juillet **49**
Conciergerie................**16**
Cour d'Honneur **64**
Cuisine St-Louis..........**17**

Dôme des Invalides **64**

Ecole Militaire **63**
Egouts (the sewers) **70**
Eiffel Tower **62–3**
Elysée Palace.........**33–4**
Equestrian Statue
  of Joan of Arc **41**
Euro Disney **70**

Fontaine de
  l'Observatoire...........**58**
Fontaine St-Michel.....**55**
Forum des Halles **44**

Galeries Lafayette.......**38**
Garden of the Palais
  Royal **39**
Gare d'Orsay
  (Palais du Louvre) **65**
Glass Pyramid **25**
Grand Arche **70**
Grand Palais **33**
Grand Véfour
  restaurant **39**

Hôtel Carnavalet........**49**
Hôtel de Rohan **51**
Hôtel de Ville..............**46**
Hôtel des Invalides......**64**
Hôtel-Dieu..................**18**
Hôtel Guénégaud **51**
Hôtel Lauzun **21**
Hôtel Salé (Musée
  Picasso).....................**50**

Ile de la Cité.........**14–20**
Ile Saint-Louis............**21**
Institut de France........**60**
Institut Pasteur **67**

Jardin des Tuileries **29**
Jardin du
  Luxembourg **58**
Jeu de Paume **31**
Jewish Quarter............**51**
Jim Morrison's grave ..**71**

La Défense...................**69**
La Géode.....................**71**
La Ruche **66**

La Villette **71**
Lac Inférieur...............**69**
Lac Supérieur..............**69**
Lapin Agile (inn) **54**
Louvre **22–8**

Maison de
  L'UNESCO................**63**
Marché aux Fleurs.......**18**
Marché aux Oiseaux....**18**
Mémorial de la
  Déportation...............**20**
Montmartre **52–4**
Montparnasse **66–8**
Monument du
  Maréchal Ney **58**
Mosquée **70**
Moulin de la Galette....**54**
Moulin-Rouge **52**
Musée Bourdelle **67**
Musée Cognacq-Jay **50**
Musée d'Orsay **65**
Musée de l'Armée........**64**
Musée de l'Homme......**62**
Musée de la Chasse **51**
Musée de la Marine.....**62**
Musée de la Poste........**61**
Musée des Arts de la
  Mode.........................**28**
Musée des Monuments
  Français **62**
Musée du Cinéma
  Henri Langlois..........**62**
Musée du
  Louvre **25–28**
Musée du Théâtre
  National de l'Opéra ..**37**
Musée du Vieux-
  Montmartre **54**
Musée Grevin..............**38**
Musée National d'Art
  Moderne **45**
Musée National du
  Moyen Age...............**56**
Musée Picasso.............**50**
Musée Rodin **65**
Musée Victor Hugo.....**49**
Museum of Municipal
  History......................**50**

Notre-Dame **18–20**

Observatoire................**71**
Opera Library **37**
Opéra...........................**37**
Opéra de la Bastille.....**49**
Orangerie....................**31**

Palais Bourbon **65**
Palais de Chaillot **61–2**

Palais de Justice **16**
Palais de l'Horloge......**24**
Palais de la Cité...........**14**
Palais du Louvre **22–5**
Palais du
  Luxembourg **58**
Palais du Trocadéro.....**61**
Palais Royal **40**
Panthéon......................**57**
Paris Conservatoire **71**
Père-Lachaise..............**71**
Petit-Palais **33**
Place de l'Hôtel
  de Ville....................**45**
Place de l'Opera **37**
Place de la Bastille **48**
Place de la
  Concorde **31**
Place de la
  République **51**
Place des Pyramides....**41**
Place des Abbesses......**52**
Place des Vosges.........**49**
Place du Châtelet.........**47**
Place du Parvis
  Notre-Dame **18**
Place du Tertre **53**
Place Pigalle...............**52**
Place St-Michel...........**55**
Place Vendôme **42**
Pont Neuf **14**
Pont au Change **47**
Préfecture de Police **17**
Printemps
  department store **38**

Quai des Orfèvres **17**
Quartier Latin........**55–60**

Rue de la Gaîté **68**
Rue de Rivoli **29**

Sacré Coeur **53–4**
Sainte-Chapelle **14**
Sorbonne **56–7**
Square St-Jacques **47**
Synagogue...................**51**

Théâtre du Châtelet **47**
Théâtre Français..........**40**
Théâtre Sarah-
  Bernhardt.................**47**
Tour d'Horloge **16**
Tour Maine-
  Montparnasse **66**
Tour St-Jacques..........**47**
Triumphal Column
  (Place Vendôme) **42**
Tuileries **24**
Tuileries Palace...........**24**